JAVA™ LOOK AND FEEL DESIGN GUIDELINES:
ADVANCED TOPICS

Please send your email feedback to us at jlfguide-at@sun.com

The Java™ Series

Lisa Friendly, Series Editor
Tim Lindholm, Technical Editor
Ken Arnold, Technical Editor of The Jini™ Technology Series
Jim Inscore, Technical Editor of The Java™ Series, Enterprise Edition

---

Ken Arnold, James Gosling, David Holmes
The Java™ Programming Language, Third Edition

Joshua Bloch
Effective Java™ Programming Language Guide

Greg Bollella, James Gosling, Ben Brosgol, Peter Dibble,
Steve Furr, David Hardin, Mark Turnbull
The Real-Time Specification for Java™

Mary Campione, Kathy Walrath, Alison Huml
*The Java™ Tutorial, Third Edition:
A Short Course on the Basics*

Mary Campione, Kathy Walrath, Alison Huml,Tutorial Team
*The Java™ Tutorial Continued:
The Rest of the JDK™*

Patrick Chan
The Java™ Developers Almanac 2000

Patrick Chan, Rosanna Lee
*The Java™ Class Libraries, Second Edition, Volume 2:
java.applet, java.awt, java.beans*

Patrick Chan, Rosanna Lee
The Java™ Class Libraries Poster, Sixth Edition, Part 1

Patrick Chan, Rosanna Lee
The Java™ Class Libraries Poster, Sixth Edition, Part 2

Patrick Chan, Rosanna Lee, Doug Kramer
*The Java™ Class Libraries, Second Edition, Volume 1:
java.io, java.lang, java.math, java.net, java.text, java.util*

Patrick Chan, Rosanna Lee, Doug Kramer
*The Java™ Class Libraries, Second Edition, Volume 1:
Supplement for the Java™ 2 Platform,
 Standard Edition, v1.2*

Kirk Chen, Li Gong
*Programming Open Service Gateways with Java™
 Embedded Server*

Zhiqun Chen
*Java Card™ Technology for Smart Cards:
Architecture and Programmer's Guide*

Li Gong
*Inside Java™ 2 Platform Security:
Architecture, API Design, and Implementation*

James Gosling, Bill Joy, Guy Steele, Gilad Bracha
The Java™ Language Specification, Second Edition

Mark Hapner, Rich Burridge, Rahul Sharma, Joseph Fialli,
Kim Haase
*Java™ Message Service API Tutorial and Reference:
Messaging for the J2EE™ Platform*

Jonni Kanerva
The Java™ FAQ

Doug Lea
*Concurrent Programming in Java™, Second Edition:
Design Principles and Patterns*

Rosanna Lee, Scott Seligman
*JNDI API Tutorial and Reference:
Building Directory-Enabled Java™ Applications*

Sheng Liang
*The Java™ Native Interface:
Programmer's Guide and Specification*

Tim Lindholm and Frank Yellin
The Java™ Virtual Machine Specification, Second Edition

Vlada Matena and Beth Stearns
*Applying Enterprise JavaBeans™:
Component-Based Development for the J2EE™ Platform*

Roger Riggs, Antero Taivalsaari, Mark VandenBrink
*Programming Wireless Devices with the Java™ 2
 Platform, Micro Edition*

Rahul Sharma, Beth Stearns, Tony Ng
*J2EE™ Connector Architecture and Enterprise Application
 Integration*

Henry Sowizral, Kevin Rushforth, and Michael Deering
The Java 3D™ API Specification, Second Edition

Sun Microsystems, Inc.
Java™ Look and Feel Design Guidelines: Advanced Topics

Kathy Walrath, Mary Campione
*The JFC Swing Tutorial:
A Guide to Constructing GUIs*

Seth White, Maydene Fisher, Rick Cattell, Graham Hamilton,
 Mark Hapner
*JDBC™ API Tutorial and Reference, Second Edition:
Universal Data Access for the Java™ 2 Platform*

Steve Wilson, Jeff Kesselman
*Java™ Platform Performance:
Strategies and Tactics*

The Jini™ Technology Series

Eric Freeman, Susanne Hupfer, Ken Arnold
JavaSpaces™ Principles, Patterns, and Practice

Jim Waldo/Jini™ Technology Team
*The Jini™ Specifications, Second Edition,
 edited by Ken Arnold*

The Java™ Series, Enterprise Edition

Rick Cattell, Jim Inscore, Enterprise Partners
*J2EE™ Technology in Practice:
Building Business Applications with the Java™ 2 Platform,
 Enterprise Edition*

Patrick Chan, Rosanna Lee
*The Java™ Class Libraries Poster, Enterprise Edition,
 version 1.2*

Nicholas Kassem, Enterprise Team
*Designing Enterprise Applications with the Java™ 2
 Platform, Enterprise Edition*

Bill Shannon, Mark Hapner, Vlada Matena, James
 Davidson, Eduardo Pelegri-Llopart, Larry Cable,
 Enterprise Team
*Java™ 2 Platform, Enterprise Edition:
 Platform and Component Specifications*

http://www.javaseries.com

JAVA™ LOOK AND FEEL DESIGN GUIDELINES:
ADVANCED TOPICS

Sun Microsystems, Inc.

Boston • San Francisco • New York • Toronto • Montreal
London • Munich • Paris • Madrid
Capetown • Sydney • Tokyo • Singapore • Mexico City

The publisher offers discounts on this book when ordered in quantity for special sales. For more information, please contact:

Addison-Wesley Professional
75 Arlington Street, Suite 300
Boston, Massachusetts 02116
U.S.A.

Text printed on recycled and acid-free paper

Library of Congress Cataloging-in-Publication Data

Java look and feel design guidelines : advanced topics/
Sun Microsystems, Inc.
    p. cm. – (Java series)
    Includes index.
    ISBN 0-201-77582-4 (alk. paper)
    1. Java (Computer program language) I. Sun Microsystems.
II. Series.

QA76.73.J38 J375 2002
005.13'3–dc21
                                                    2001056053

 Please Recycle   Adobe PostScript™

CONTENTS

PREFACE

Java Look and Feel Design Guidelines: Advanced Topics provides guidelines for anyone designing user interfaces for **applications** written in the Java™ programming language. In particular, this book offers design guidelines for applications that use the Java look and feel. This book supplements *Java Look and Feel Design Guidelines*, 2d ed. For details on that book, see "Related Books" on page xiv.

Although some topics in *Java Look and Feel Design Guidelines: Advanced Topics* apply only to certain types of applications, most topics apply to all applications that use the Java look and feel.

Who Should Use This Book
Primarily, this book addresses the **designer** who chooses an application's user-interface elements, lays them out in a set of components, and designs the user interaction model for an application. This book should also prove useful for software developers, technical writers, graphic artists, production and marketing specialists, and testers who help create applications that use the Java look and feel.

Java Look and Feel Design Guidelines: Advanced Topics focuses on design issues and human-computer interaction in the context of the Java look and feel. For information about technical aspects of the Java Foundation Classes (**JFC**), visit the JFC and Swing Connection web sites:

- http://java.sun.com/products/jfc
- http://java.sun.com/products/jfc/tsc

The guidelines in this book are appropriate for GUI applications that run on personal computers and network computers. These guidelines are not intended for software that runs on consumer electronic devices, such as wireless telephones or personal digital assistants (PDAs).

How to Use This Book
This book is intended to be read in its entirety or to be consulted as a reference on particular topics. The information in this book is easier to understand if you first read *Java Look and Feel Design Guidelines*, 2d ed. If you read only particular topics in this book, you should also see any corresponding topics in that book.

This book assumes that you are familiar with the terms and concepts in *Java Look and Feel Design Guidelines*, 2d ed., which is available in printed form at bookstores and as hypertext at the following web address:

    http://java.sun.com/products/jlf

In addition, this book assumes that you are using the default Java look and feel theme, as described in Chapter 4 of *Java Look and Feel Design Guidelines*, 2d ed.

What Is in This Book   This book contains two main parts— "General Topics" and "Special Topics."

Part One, "General Topics," consists of chapters whose user interface guidelines apply to most applications.

- **Chapter 1, "Introduction,"** explains why a consistent look and feel is important in applications and describes characteristics of well-designed applications.
- **Chapter 2, "Windows,"** defines user-interface objects and then describes various types of windows. In addition, the chapter describes how to choose the right window type, design window elements, set the state of windows, and handle multiple windows.
- **Chapter 3, "Menus,"** provides guidelines for designing menu elements, common menus (such as File, Edit, and Help), and contextual menus. The chapter also provides guidelines for assigning mnemonics and keyboard shortcuts to menu items.
- **Chapter 4, "Behavior,"** discusses modes of user interaction, multiple selection, filtering, searching, and tool tips.
- **Chapter 5, "Idioms,"** describes how to use sets of JFC components to achieve a standardized appearance and behavior. In particular, the chapter discusses idioms for tables, text fields, lists, and hierarchies of user-interface objects.
- **Chapter 6, "Responsiveness,"** discusses characteristics of responsive applications, describes how responsiveness relates to performance and to response delay, explains how to measure response delay, and describes ways to improve responsiveness and provide operational feedback to users.

Part Two, "Special Topics," consists of chapters whose guidelines apply only to applications that include wizards or alarms.

- **Chapter 7, "Wizards,"** introduces wizards and then describes how to decide whether your users need a wizard, how to design the layout and behavior of wizards, and what other factors to consider when designing wizards.

■ **Chapter 8, "Events and Alarms,"** defines the terms "event" and "alarm" and then provides information on how to display alarm views (representations of alarms) and how to manipulate alarm views (for example, by sorting them at a user's request).

The rest of the book consists of a glossary and index.

■ **Glossary** defines important terms used in this book. Glossary terms are in boldface throughout the book.

What Is Not in This Book

This book does not provide detailed discussions of human interface design principles or the design process, nor does it present information about **task analysis**—an essential concept in user interface design. For resources on these topics, see "Related Books" on page xiv and "Related Books and Web Sites" in *Java Look and Feel Design Guidelines*, 2d ed.

Many of this book's guidelines can be applied to applications that use the Java look and feel to display text in any language. However, the usability of the book's guidelines and examples has been tested only with languages in which users read left to right. If you are designing for users who read right to left, use your judgment to decide whether this book's guidelines regarding layout are appropriate for your application.

Graphic Conventions

The screen shots in this book illustrate the use of JFC components in applications with the Java look and feel. Except where noted, measurements called out in screen shots are in pixels.

Throughout the text, symbols call your attention to Java look and feel design guidelines and to tips for implementing them.

Java Look and Feel Standards

Requirements for the consistent appearance and compatible behavior of Java look and feel applications. To conform with the Java look and feel, applications must meet these requirements.

Java look and feel standards promote consistency and ease of use in applications. In addition, they support the creation of applications that are accessible to all users, including users with physical and cognitive limitations. These guidelines require you to take actions that go beyond the provided appearance and behavior of the JFC components.

⊞⊃ **Implementation Tips**   Technical information and useful tips of particular interest to the programmers who are implementing your application design.

Related Books   The preface to *Java Look and Feel Design Guidelines*, 2d ed., cites many references on topics such as fundamental principles of human interface design, design issues for specific (or multiple) platforms, and issues relating to internationalization and **accessibility**. This section does not repeat those references; instead, it lists only books to which this book refers.

- Sun Microsystems, Inc. *Java Look and Feel Design Guidelines*, 2d ed., Addison-Wesley, 2001. This book provides essential information for anyone involved in creating cross-platform GUI (graphical user interface) applications and applets in the Java programming language. In particular, the book offers design guidelines for software that uses the Java look and feel.

- Hackos, JoAnn T., and Janice C. Redish. *User and Task Analysis for Interface Design*. John Wiley & Sons, Inc., 1998. This book explains how to observe and interview users to gather the information you need to design your application.

- Johnson, Jeff. *GUI Bloopers: Don'ts and Do's for Software Developers and Web Designers*. Morgan Kaufman, 2000. This book provides examples of poor design in windows, inconsistent use of labels, and lack of parallelism in visual layout and grammar. The writer develops principles for achieving lucidity and harmony of look and feel.

- Wilson, Steve, and Jeff Kesselman. *Java Platform Performance: Strategies and Tactics*. Addison-Wesley, 2000. Intended to help software developers write high-performance software for the Java platform, this book describes the various qualities known as performance and describes how to attain and measure them.

PART I: GENERAL TOPICS

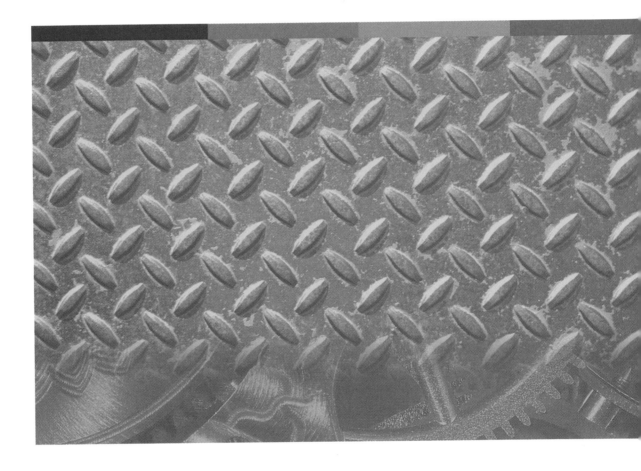

1: INTRODUCTION

An application's usability depends on its appearance and behavior—its **look and feel**. A consistent look and feel helps users learn an application faster and use it more efficiently. In addition, a consistent look and feel helps users learn other applications that share that look and feel.

This book provides guidelines for designing applications with the **Java look and feel**. All the guidelines are intended to help you create a well-designed application.

Well-designed applications have the following characteristics:

- Logical organization
- Scalability
- Predictability
- Responsiveness
- Efficiency

The rest of this chapter describes each of these characteristics, why each is important, and which parts of this book relate to each characteristic.

Logical Organization

Applications that use the Java look and feel consist of user interface components displayed in windows. The way that you organize your application into windows and components should be consistent with the logical divisions that users perceive in their tasks. For example, a logically organized email application might include:

- A window for reading received messages, each of which is an object
- A window for composing messages, with components such as text fields for addressees, a text area for the message, and a button for sending the message

Logical organization is especially important in applications that display many objects in several windows. For example, an application for managing a large network might display:

- Windows displaying sets of network domains
- Views (such as icons or table entries) of each domain's nodes
- Views of each node's properties (for example, its network address)

Chapter 2 discusses how to choose the correct types of windows for different types of user interaction. Within a window, usability often depends on whether menus are organized logically. Chapter 3 describes how to design menus.

Scalability

Applications sometimes need to display widely varying numbers of user interface objects. For example, in an application that monitors the computers of a growing corporation, the number of objects representing computers at a particular site might increase rapidly. When looking for a particular object in a window representing that site, a user might need to view 15 objects in one month or 1500 the next. The user interface of such an application should be scalable. In other words, it should enable users to find, view, and manipulate widely varying numbers of objects.

This book discusses several ways to make your application's user interface more scalable. For example, Chapter 4 describes filtering and searching—features that enhance an application's ability to manipulate large sets of objects.

Predictability

To learn new parts of an application, users often rely on their experience with the application's other parts. Slight inconsistencies between the look and feel of different parts can frustrate users and reduce their productivity. Chapter 5 describes ways to group JFC components into reusable units that promote predictability in your application.

Responsiveness

Responsiveness is an application's ability to keep up with users. It is often cited as the strongest factor in users' satisfaction with applications. Chapter 6 describes techniques for measuring and improving your application's responsiveness.

Efficiency

To provide maximum usability, your application must be efficient. An application's logical organization, scalability, predictability, and responsiveness all contribute to its efficiency.

Efficiency is especially important if users' tasks are complex and time-consuming. User aids, such as wizards, can help new users and experienced users work efficiently. Chapter 7 describes how to design wizards that are as efficient as other user-interface designs.

In applications that monitor and manage real-time systems — such as large computer systems and networks — a user's ability to respond efficiently to alarms can sometimes prevent major system failures. Chapter 8 discusses how to design applications that enable users to handle alarms efficiently.

2: WINDOWS

The Java platform provides several types of **windows**, each for a different type of interaction. To help you choose appropriate windows types for your application, this chapter:

- Introduces objects and properties, which are displayed in windows
- Provides an overview of window types
- Explains how to choose the correct window type
- Describes various window types in detail
- Describes how to title windows and set their state
- Provides guidelines about using multiple document interfaces

This chapter supplements Chapters 7 and 8 of *Java Look and Feel Design Guidelines*, 2d ed.

In this chapter, the **dialog box** window type is subdivided into **action windows** and **property windows**, both described here.

For information about using menus in windows, see Chapter 3.

Windows, Objects, and Properties

Windows can display user interface objects. An **object** is a logical entity that an application displays and a user manipulates—for example, a document or paragraph in a word-processing application. User interface objects do not necessarily correspond to Java programming language objects in an application's code. User interface objects represent data or other parts of a user's tasks.

User interface objects have characteristics called **properties**. For example, a paragraph might have a property that determines whether it is indented. Users can view or set the values of properties.

Applications can display a single object in more than one **view**. For example, at a user's request, an application might display the same objects as list items, table entries, or **icons**, as shown in Figure 1.

FIGURE 1   Different Views of the Same Objects

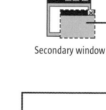

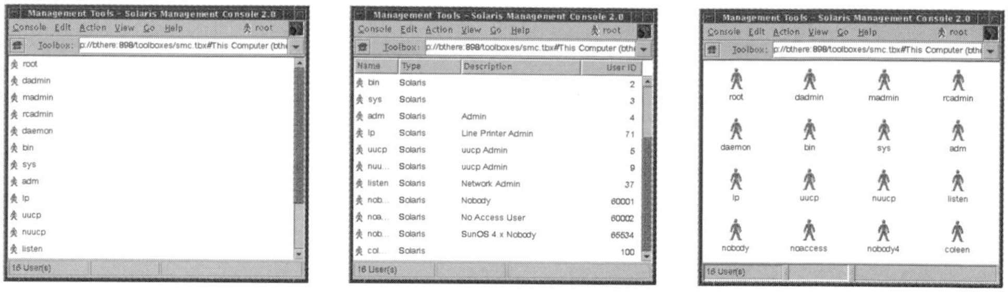

Overview of Window Types

The Java platform provides the following basic window types:

- **Plain windows**
- **Utility windows**
- **Primary windows**
- **Secondary windows**

Figure 2 shows these window types and their subtypes.

FIGURE 2   Window Types

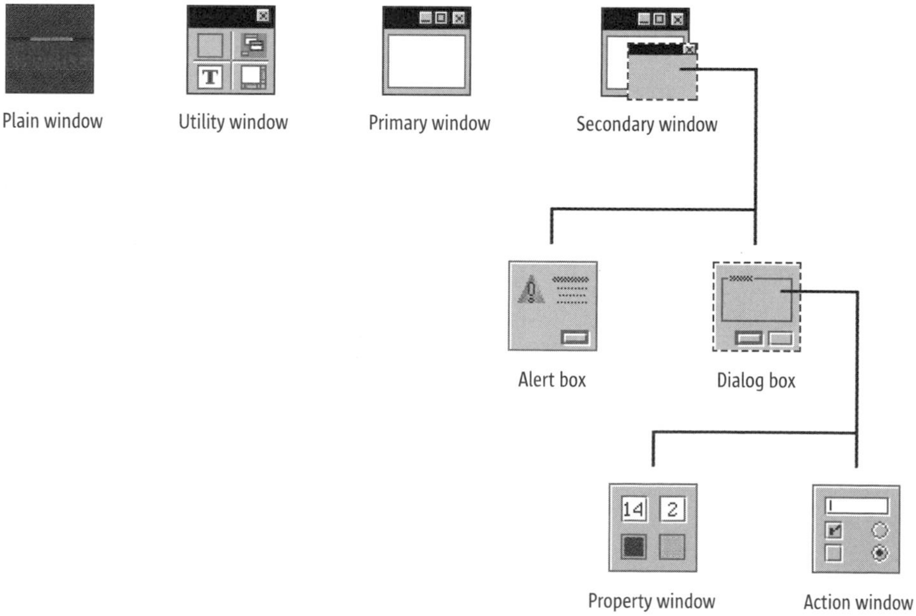

Plain window   Utility window   Primary window   Secondary window

Alert box   Dialog box

Property window   Action window

Table 1 lists each window type and describes its intended use.

TABLE 1   Window Types and Intended Use

Window Type	Intended Use
Plain window	Typically, displays a splash screen, which appears briefly in the time between when an application starts and when the application's main window appears.
Utility window	Displays a set of tools (for example, the drawing tools in a graphics program), or enables other user interaction that can affect a primary window.
Primary window	Represents an object or a set of objects. A primary window can have any number of dependent, or secondary, windows. For more information, see "Primary Windows" on page 10.
Secondary window	An **alert box** or a dialog box:
	Alert box—Enables brief interaction with a user—for example, to display error messages or warn of potential problems. For more information, see "Alerting Users After an Object's State Changes" on page 30.
	Dialog box—A property window or an action window: • Property window—Enables a user to display or set the properties of one or more objects, typically objects in the parent window (which opened the property window). For more information, see "Property Windows" on page 12. • Action window—Prompts a user for information needed to perform an action (such as opening a file). The user requested the action from the parent window. Action windows are not for displaying or setting properties of objects. For more information, see "Action Windows" on page 22.

Window Types for Objects, Properties, and Actions

A window's intended use determines its correct window type. Choosing the correct window type is especially important when displaying objects or properties.

Only two window types are intended for displaying objects and their properties:

- Primary windows
- Property windows

You can use an action window to let users perform actions on an object. In addition, you can enable users to perform actions on objects by providing drop-down menus or equivalent **controls**.

To represent an object or a set of objects, use a primary window. To represent an object's properties, use a property window. Use these window types only for these purposes.

When providing a window for performing actions on an object, use an action window. However, do not use an action window to display or set the properties of an object. Use a property window instead.

Primary Windows

A primary window is the main window in which a user interacts with a document or data. An application can have one or more primary windows, each of which a user can manipulate independently.

A primary window represents an object (such as an email message) or a set of objects (such as all the messages in a mail window). For information about representing the properties of objects, see "Property Windows" on page 12.

Primary windows contain a **title bar** and, optionally, a **menu bar**, **toolbar**, and **status bar**, as shown in Figure 3.

FIGURE 3   Elements of a Primary Window

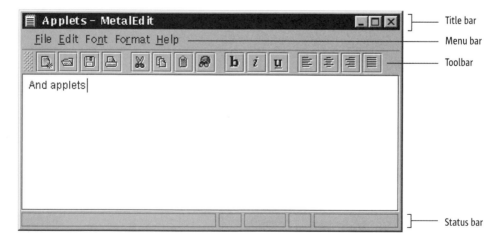

Title Bars in Primary Windows

The title bar of a primary window displays text that includes the name of the object, or set of objects, that the window represents. Figure 4 shows a typical title bar for a primary window.

FIGURE 4   Title Bar of a Primary Window

▤ **Engineering Models – MetalEdit**   ▬ ▢ ✕

For more information about window titles, see Chapter 7 of *Java Look and Feel Design Guidelines*, 2d ed. In addition, see "Window Titles for Identically Named Objects and Views" on page 26 of this book.

☕ In primary windows, begin the window title text with the name of the object or set of objects that the window represents, followed by a space, a hyphen, another space, and the application name.

Toolbars in Primary Windows   Primary windows can contain a toolbar, as shown in Figure 5.

FIGURE 5   Toolbar of a Primary Window

A toolbar can contain any combination of the following controls:

- **Command buttons**—for example, a button for printing or searching

- Controls for choosing modes of interaction—for example, buttons for choosing painting tools in a graphics application

- Controls that dynamically change and display an object's property values—for example, in a word-processing program, a button that both italicizes the current text and shows that the current text is italicized

☕ If users can access an action from a toolbar, provide keyboard access to that action as well. Alternatively, provide an equivalent action that is keyboard accessible. For example, if you provide a toolbar control for printing text, you might also provide a menu item for printing text. Toolbar controls can differ from their corresponding menu items—but only in that the toolbar control uses default values, whereas the menu item opens an action window.

☕ When providing a keyboard-accessible alternative to a toolbar control, ensure that the alternative has at least the capabilities of the toolbar control.

☕ Omit all toolbar controls from the **keyboard traversal order** so that expert users can navigate more easily. If a user presses the Tab key to move keyboard focus in a window, do not move focus to toolbar controls.

☕ Provide a tool tip for each toolbar control, especially if the control has no label. (For more information about tool tips, see "Tool Tips" on page 62.)

Status Bars in Primary Windows
The bottom of primary windows can include a status bar, as shown in Figure 6.

FIGURE 6   Status Bar at the Bottom of a Primary Window

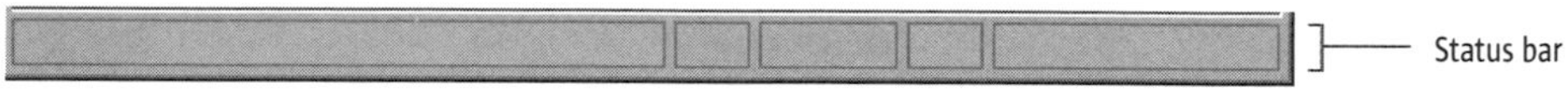

└─── Status bar

You can use the status bar to display status messages and read-only information about the object that the window represents.

☕ In a window's status bar, ensure that each message fits the available space when the window is at its default size.

☕ To avoid displaying obsolete information in a window's status bar, clear each status message when the next user action occurs in that window.

Property Windows
A property window is a dialog box in which users can display or change values of one or more object properties.

Property Window Characteristics
A property window has four main behavioral characteristics—one from each of the following pairs:

- **Modal** or **modeless**
- **Single-use** or **multiple-use**
- **Dedicated** or **non-dedicated**
- **Inspecting** or **non-inspecting**

This section discusses only the following characteristics:

- Dedicated
- Non-dedicated
- Inspecting
- Non-inspecting

For a discussion of the remaining characteristics, see Chapter 8 of *Java Look and Feel Design Guidelines*, 2d ed.

Table 2 describes each main behavioral characteristic that can apply to property windows.

TABLE 2   Property Window Characteristics

Characteristic	Description
Modal	Prevents a user from interacting with other windows in the current application.
Modeless	Does not prevent a user from interacting with other windows in the current application.
Single-use	Intended for users who are likely to perform only one operation with the dialog box before dismissing it.
Multiple-use	Intended for users who are likely to perform more than one operation with the dialog box before dismissing it.
Dedicated	Affects only objects already selected when the property window opened.
Non-dedicated	Affects currently selected objects, even if the current selection changes.
Inspecting	Displays a continuously updated view of the property values for the currently selected object, even if the values change.
Non-inspecting	Displays a static view, or snapshot, of the selected object's property values.

Only a few combinations of the characteristics in Table 2 are recommended, so choosing the correct property window characteristics is simpler than it might seem. This section describes how to make the correct choices. Later sections describe each property window characteristic in detail.

Figure 7 shows a primary window, an inspecting property window, and a non-inspecting property window.

FIGURE 7   Property Windows and a Primary Window

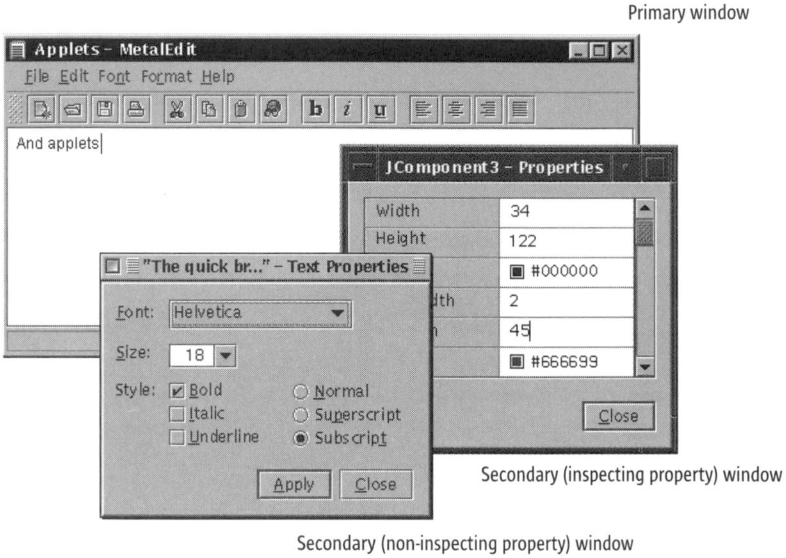

Primary window

Secondary (inspecting property) window

Secondary (non-inspecting property) window

For information about positioning a property window in relation to its parent window, see "Positioning Secondary Windows" on page 29.

Choosing the Correct Property Window Characteristics   Before choosing characteristics for your application's property windows, consider how users should interact with each window. A property window's intended use determines its correct window characteristics. Figure 8 helps you choose the correct characteristics for property windows.

FIGURE 8   Steps for Choosing Property Window Characteristics

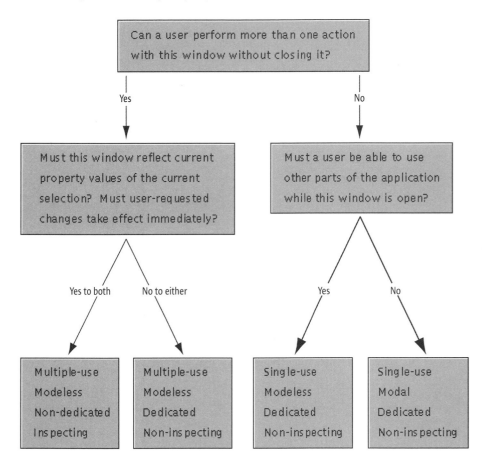

Of the sets of property window characteristics in Figure 8, only two sets are typically used in applications. Table 3 provides examples of property windows whose characteristics match those of the typical sets.

TABLE 3   Examples of Typical Property Windows

Property Window Characteristics	Example
Multiple-use, modeless, non-dedicated, inspecting	The small windows for choosing colors or layers in graphics applications such as Adobe® Photoshop software.
Single-use, modeless, dedicated, non-inspecting	The Preferences dialog box of a typical application.

Dedicated and Non-Dedicated Property Windows   A dedicated property window affects only objects already selected when the property window opened. Changing the selection while a dedicated property window is open does not change which objects the property window affects.

In contrast, a non-dedicated property window affects only objects currently selected—even if the selection changes while the property window is open. In other words, a non-dedicated property window affects whichever objects are currently selected when a user clicks the window's OK button or Apply button. In a non-dedicated property window, a user can change which objects the window affects. To do so, the user can select different objects while the window is open.

Inspecting and Non-Inspecting Property Windows   Property windows are inspecting or non-inspecting, depending on:

- How current their displayed information is
- When a user's changes take effect

Inspecting Property Windows   An inspecting property window is a dialog box that both:

- Displays a continuously updated view of the property values for the selected object, and

- Enables a user to change the displayed property values (and the selected object) immediately

Figure 9 shows an inspecting property window.

FIGURE 9   Inspecting Property Window

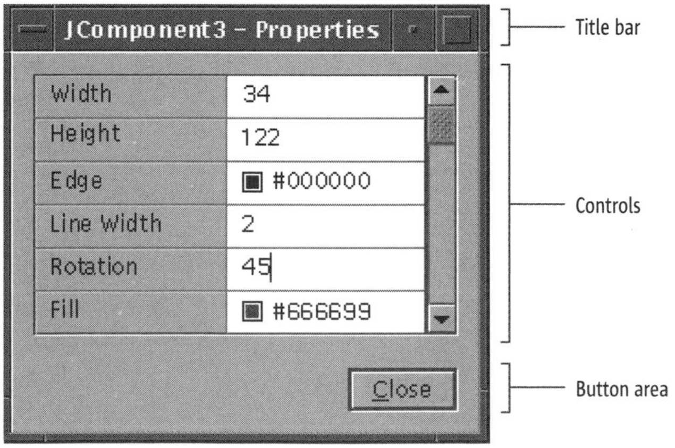

In inspecting property windows, a user does not click an OK button or Apply button to apply changes. The application applies changes automatically.

An inspecting property window displays the values of the selected object. If a user changes the selection, the values in the property window also change immediately to reflect the newly selected object. An inspecting property window continuously updates its view of an object's property values, even if those values change outside a user's control. Most inspecting property windows are modeless.

If your application has many types of objects, avoid creating a separate inspecting property window for each type. Instead, create a single inspecting property window whose contents change depending on the properties of the selected object.

If users need to update two or more interdependent property values, do not provide an inspecting property window. Instead, provide a non-inspecting property window, thereby ensuring that changes to interdependent properties occur at the same time.

Here is an example of why inspecting property windows are inappropriate for updating interdependent property values. An application has a Customer object for which users can enter an address that includes a city and country—such as Paris, France. As a user types the address, the Customer object automatically verifies that the specified city (Paris) is in the specified country (France).

In an inspecting property window, if a user tries to change the city name from Paris to Tokyo, the Customer object rejects the change because the user has not changed the country name from France to Japan. If the user then tries to change the country name, the change is again rejected, because the city name has not been changed from Paris to Tokyo.

Non-Inspecting Property Windows   A non-inspecting property window is a property window that displays a static view, or snapshot, of the selected object's property values—accurate as of the time that the property window opened. Figure 10 shows a non-inspecting property window.

FIGURE 10   Non-Inspecting Property Window

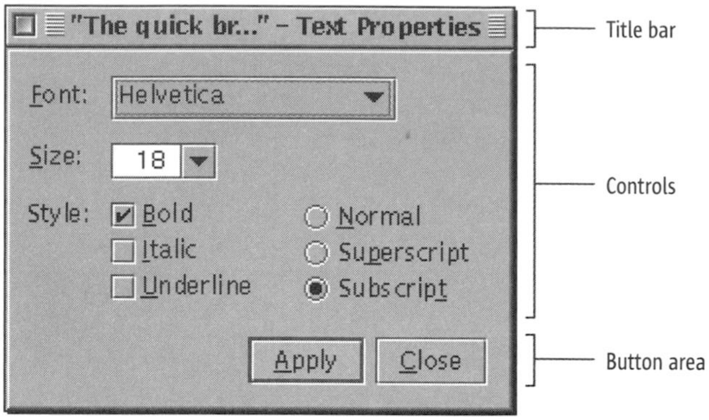

Non-inspecting property windows are particularly useful when a user needs to update several interdependent values at the same time.

If a user changes property values in a non-inspecting property window, those changes take effect only if the user clicks the window's OK button or Apply button. Changes that take place beyond the user's control are not reflected in the window until it opens again.

NOTE – If your application's objects can change outside a user's control, alert the user to any such changes. For more information, see "Alerting Users After an Object's State Changes" on page 30.

Behavior and Layout of Property Windows

For property windows, the correct behavior and command-button layout depend on the window's characteristics. This section provides guidelines for the behavior and layout of property windows.

☕ Place no menu, toolbar, or status bar in property windows.

☕ To enable users to open a property window, place an item labeled Properties on the *Object* menu, if there is one. (*Object* stands for the type of the object whose properties the window displays—for example, Document.) If your application has no *Object* menu, place the Properties item on the Edit menu. Label the item *Object* Properties if the Edit menu also contains items for other property windows.

Title Text in Property Windows   Property windows include title text, displayed in the title bar, as shown in Figure 11.

FIGURE 11   Title Text in the Title Bar of a Property Window

📋 **SuperRivet – Alloy Properties**   _ ▢ ☒

Regardless of a property window's characteristics, the title text consists of the following items, in order:

1. The name of the object that the window represents

2. A hyphen, preceded by one space and followed by another

3. The name of the command that opened the window

In Figure 11, the window represents an object named SuperRivet. The command that opened the window is Alloy Properties.

☕ In property windows, format the title text as *Object Name - Command*, as shown in Figure 11. *Object Name* stands for the name of the currently displayed object. Precede the hyphen by one space and follow it by one space. *Command* stands for the name of the command that opened the property window.

☕ If a user might not know which application created a particular property window, include the application's name in that window's title text. Format the title text like this: *Object Name - Command - Application Name*. (Precede each hyphen by one space and follow it by one space.)

☕ In the title text of inspecting property windows, update the current object's name each time you update the window's contents.

Command Buttons in Non-Inspecting Property Windows   Table 4 describes the command buttons you can place in non-inspecting property windows.

TABLE 4   Command Buttons for Non-Inspecting Property Windows

Button	Description
Apply	Updates the properties of the associated object.
Reset	Discards any changes made in the window since the last "apply" action. The Reset command then refills the window's fields with the values from the associated object.
OK	Updates the properties of the associated object and then closes the window.

TABLE 4   Command Buttons for Non-Inspecting Property Windows *(Continued)*

Button	Description
Close	Closes the property window but not the application. If a user has changed the values in the window but has not applied them, the Close button opens an alert box containing the following text: "Your changes have not been saved. To save the changes, click Apply. To discard the changes, click Discard. To cancel your Close request, click Cancel."
Cancel	Works like the Close button, except that the Cancel button does not display an alert box before discarding changes.
Help	Displays help text in another window while leaving the property window open.

Before deciding which command buttons to place in a non-inspecting property window, estimate how many times a user needs to use the window before closing it.

If a user will use a property window only once before closing it, then place an OK and a Cancel button — in that order — at the bottom right of the window, as shown in Figure 12.

FIGURE 12   Required Buttons for a Single-Use Property Window

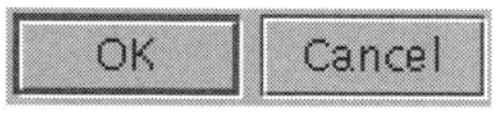

Optionally, you can add a Help button to the right of the Cancel button, as shown in Figure 13.

FIGURE 13   Required and Optional Buttons for a Single-Use Property Window

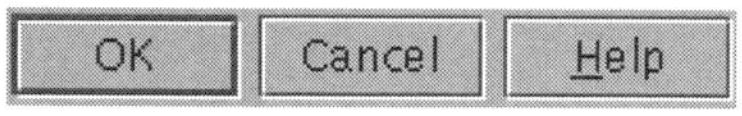

If a user will use a property window repeatedly before closing it, place an Apply and a Close button — in that order — at the bottom right of the window, as shown in Figure 14.

FIGURE 14   Required Buttons for a Repeated-Use Property Window

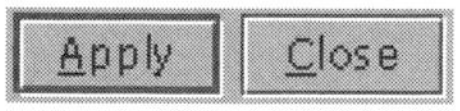

Optionally, you can place a Reset button between the Apply button and the Close button, and place a Help button to the right of the Close button, as shown in Figure 15.

FIGURE 15   Required and Optional Buttons for a Repeated-Use Property Window

The following guidelines apply only to non-inspecting property windows.

☕ Place either an OK button or an Apply button in non-inspecting property windows.

☕ Make the OK button or the Apply button the default command button. (For more information about default command buttons, see Chapter 10 of *Java Look and Feel Design Guidelines*, 2d ed.)

☕ Place the dismissal button to the right of the OK button or Apply button.

☕ If a non-inspecting property window has an OK button, label its dismissal button Cancel. Otherwise, label the dismissal button Close.

☕ Ensure that clicking the title bar's close-window control has the same effect as clicking the window's Close or Cancel button.

☕ Open an alert box if a user clicks the Close button before applying changes entered in the window. In the alert box (which includes a Discard button), display the following text: "Your changes have not been saved. To save the changes, click Apply. To discard the changes, click Discard. To cancel your Close request, click Cancel."

☕ If a non-inspecting property window has an Apply button, ensure that clicking the Apply button updates the associated object, using the current values from the property window.

☕ If a non-inspecting property window has an OK button, ensure that clicking the OK button updates the properties values of the associated object and then closes the window.

☕ If a non-inspecting property window needs a Reset button, place that button between the window's Apply and Close buttons.

☕ Ensure that clicking the Reset button performs the following operations, in order:

1. Discards any changes made in that window since it opened, or since the last "apply" operation

2. Refills the window's fields with the current values of its associated object

Command Buttons in Inspecting Property Windows   In inspecting property windows, place a Close button at the bottom right of the window. Optionally, place a Help button to the right of the Close button.

The following guidelines apply only to inspecting property windows.

☕ Ensure that clicking the Close button immediately closes the window.

☕ Ensure that clicking the title bar's close-window control has the same effect as clicking the window's Close button.

☕ Some controls do not immediately send their updates to the object being inspected. (For example, a text field does not send its updated text until it has lost input focus.) In inspecting property windows, send all pending updates to the window's object when a user clicks the window's Close button or close-window control.

Action Windows   Action windows are dialog boxes that request information for completing an action. Open an action window if a user activates a menu command or command button that requires additional user input to complete an action. Figure 16 shows an action window.

FIGURE 16   Action Window

As shown in Figure 16, an action window contains:

- Title bar
- Controls
- Button area

An action window has no menu, toolbar, or status bar.

The label of a menu command or command button that opens an action window ends with an **ellipsis** (...). The ellipsis means that the command requires additional user input.

Like property windows, action windows can be:

- Modal or modeless
- Single-use or multiple-use

For more information about these characteristics, see Chapter 8 of *Java Look and Feel Design Guidelines*, 2d ed.

For information about positioning an action window in relation to its parent window, see "Positioning Secondary Windows" on page 29.

☕ Ensure that an action window has no menu, toolbar, or status bar.

☕ Place an ellipsis (...) at the end of the label for a menu command or command button that opens an action window.

Title Text in Action Windows

The title text of an action window helps users understand the window's purpose. An action window's title text includes:

- The name of the object that the action window affects (if you know the name)
- The name of the menu item or command button that opened the action window (omitting any trailing ellipsis)

Figure 17 shows the title text of an action window opened from a Print menu item. The window affects an object named `MySalesForecast`.

FIGURE 17 Title Text in the Title Bar of an Action Window

If an action window enables a user to create an object, the window's title text cannot include that object's name because the object does not yet exist. Figure 18 shows the title text of such an action window, opened from a New Rivet menu item.

FIGURE 18 Title Text of an Action Window That Creates a New Object

In Figure 18, the title text shows only the name of the menu item that opened the action window.

☕ In the title text of an action window, include the name of the menu item or command button that opened the action window. Omit the name's trailing ellipsis, if there is one.

☕ If an action window affects an existing object, format the title text like this: *Object Name - Menu Item*. (Precede the hyphen by one space and follow it by one space.)

☕ If an action window creates a new object, make the window's title text the name of the menu item or command button that opened the window.

☕ If a user might not recognize the source of a particular action window, format the title text like this: *Object Name - Menu Item - Application Name*. (Precede each hyphen by one space and follow it by one space.)

☕ In a modeless action window, ensure that the title text always reflects the object that the window affects.

Command Buttons in Action Windows

Action windows have the following command buttons (in left-to-right order):

- One or more command buttons that perform actions
- One dismissal button
- One Help button (optional)

The command buttons are right-justified in the window's button area, as shown in Figure 19.

FIGURE 19   Command Buttons in an Action Window (Multiple-Use)

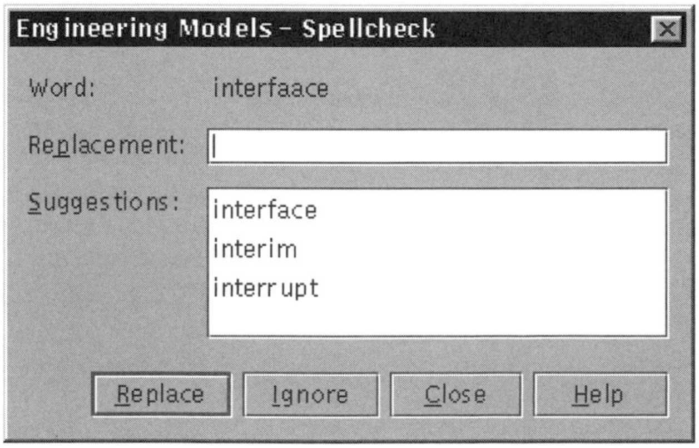

An action window's leftmost command button performs an action using values from the window's controls. For example, in Figure 19, the Replace button performs an action using the value that the user enters in the input field labeled Replacement.

The Help button, if there is one, is always rightmost in the button area, as in Figure 19. (For more information about the Help button, see Chapter 8 of *Java Look and Feel Design Guidelines*, 2d ed.)

An action window's rightmost command button (or the one directly to the left of the Help button) closes the window.

If an action window has additional buttons, each one performs a different action using the values from the window's controls. The additional buttons are between the leftmost and rightmost buttons.

The correct labels to use for an action window's command buttons depend on whether the window is for single-use or multiple-use:

- In a single-use action window, you can label the first button OK— although a more specific label, such as Print, is better. The window's dismissal button must be labeled Cancel.

- In a multiple-use action window, you should assign the first button a meaningful label, such as Replace. The window's dismissal button must be labeled Close, as in Figure 19.

In action windows with two or more buttons that can perform an action, each button needs a unique action-specific label. Do not label a button OK in such a window.

☕ Ensure that each action window has (in left-to-right order) one or more command buttons that perform actions, one dismissal button, and, optionally, a Help button.

☕ Action windows can be single-use or multiple-use. In a single-use action window, ensure that all command buttons (except the Help button) perform their action and then close the window. In a multiple-use action window, ensure that all command buttons except the Close button perform their action and leave the window open.

☕ In a single-use action window, label the dismissal button Cancel. In a multiple-use action window, label the dismissal button Close.

☕ If users can perform only one action from a single-use action window, label the window's command button OK, or preferably, provide a more specific label. However, if the window has more than one button that can cause an action, do not label any button OK. Instead, provide a more specific label for each button.

☕ In an action window, ensure that clicking the dismissal button immediately discards all data entered in that window.

☕ In an action window, ensure that clicking the title bar's close-window control has the same effect as clicking the window's dismissal button.

Window Titles for Identically Named Objects and Views

In applications with multiple windows, each window title should be unique. This section helps you create unique window titles for:

- Multiple windows representing different objects whose names are identical

- Multiple windows representing different views of the same object

The title text of a primary window should be in the following format:

Document or *Object Name - Application Name*

Figure 20 illustrates the conventions for titling windows that represent identically named objects or multiple views of the same object.

FIGURE 20   Window Titles for Identically Named Objects and for Multiple Views

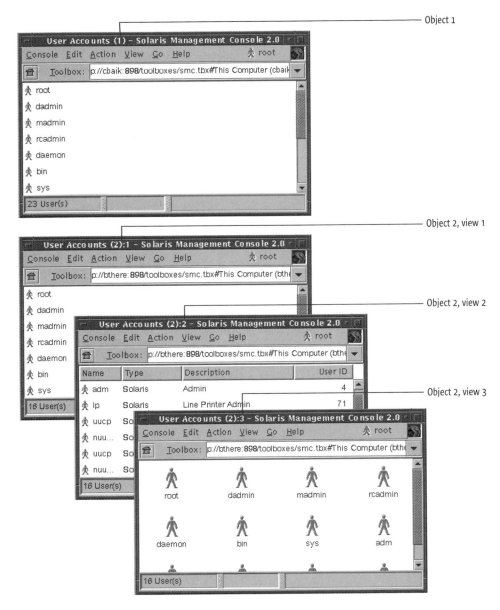

In primary windows that display identically named objects or views, the window title includes a suffix to the *Object Name*. However, the suffix is not part of the *Object Name*. For example, in Object 2, view 1, of Figure 20, the suffix "(2):1" is not part of "User Accounts"—the *Object Name*.

Window Titles for Identically Named Objects   Applications can display more than one window at a time. As a result, different windows can display objects whose names are identical. For example, two windows might each display a different document named `Report`. To avoid confusion and to help users distinguish between such windows, use the following guideline.

☕ If two or more objects have the same name, make their names unique in window titles by appending a space and the suffix (*n*) to the *Object Name* in each window's title text—where *n* is an increasing integer.

Window Titles for Multiple Views of the Same Object   Typically, applications show a particular object in only one window at a time. Sometimes, however, an application needs to show two or more views of the same object in different windows.

For example, at a user's request, an application might show the contents of a folder or directory as a list in one window and as a set of icons in a different window. In such windows, the correct format for the *Object Name* in the title text depends on whether the window is a primary window, as described in the following guidelines.

☕ If multiple primary windows show views of the same object, distinguish each of the windows by appending the suffix :*n* to the object name in the window title—for example, Report:2. (The letter *n* stands for an increasing integer.)

☕ Do not place a view number in the title bar of property windows.

☕ In action windows, place a view number in the title bar only if the action produces a different result in different views.

☕ If your application displays multiple objects with the same name and multiple views of the same object, place the view number after the duplicate-name identifier in each window title—for example, Report (2):3.

Setting the State of Windows and Objects   A typical
window or object has properties whose value can change—for example, its screen position and size. For each window or object, the set of current values for all its changeable characteristics is known as its **state**. Applications often need to initialize or restore the state of a window or object. This section provides guidelines related to the state of windows and objects.

Positioning Secondary Windows   When displaying a secondary window for the first time, applications should position that window in relation to its parent window, as shown in Figure 21.

FIGURE 21   Secondary Window Correctly Positioned in a Primary Window

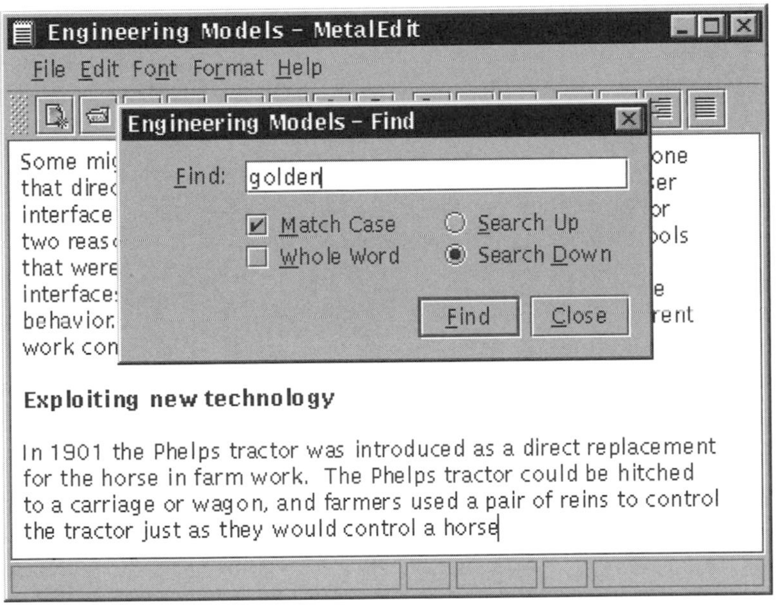

In Figure 21, the secondary window is at the **golden mean** of the parent window—a point directly on the parent's vertical midline and slightly above its horizontal midline. A secondary window centered on its parent's golden mean is generally considered more visually pleasing than the same window centered on parent's exact center.

When a secondary window opens for the first time, ensure that it is at the golden mean of its parent window. That is, ensure that the secondary window is both:

■ Centered on the vertical midline of its parent window
■ Positioned so that its top is *n* pixels below the top of the parent window

The value of *n* can be derived from the following equation, in which *h* is the height of the parent window:

$$n = h - \left(\frac{h}{1.618}\right)$$

☕ When closing and reopening a secondary window during a single application session, reopen that window where it was when it closed most recently. (Alert boxes are an exception. Always reopen an alert box at its initial position.)

Restoring the State of Property Windows   Users can change a property window's state by several means—for example, by rearranging the window's tabbed panes or other organizing elements.

☕ If a user reopens a property window after closing it during the same application session, restore that window's state. In other words, make the window look exactly as it did when the user last closed it—especially if the user has manipulated the window's components.

Alerting Users After an Object's State Changes   In some applications, an object's state can change outside a user's control—even while the user is editing the object's property window.

☕ If the state of an object changes while a user is editing that object, display an alert box if the user tries to apply changes to the object. In the alert box, inform the user that the object's state has changed.

☕ In alert boxes for informing users of object-state changes, provide text at least as specific as this:

Object Name changed while you were editing it. To update it with the values you entered, click Update. To discard the values you entered and use the new ones instead, click Discard. To cancel your attempt to edit this object, click Cancel.

Replace *Object Name* with the actual name of the changed object. If your application can detect how the object changed, display text that describes the change precisely.

Multiple Document Interfaces   Avoid designing a Multiple Document Interface (MDI) application—an application in which primary windows are represented as **internal windows** inside a **backing window**.

Many users have trouble manipulating the windows of MDI applications. In addition, an MDI application's main window can sometimes obscure a user's view of other applications.

☕ Use no internal windows in your application.

3: MENUS

In most applications, menus are one of the main ways that users issue commands. To provide maximum usability, menus must be logically ordered and easily accessible.

This chapter helps you design usable menus. It provides guidelines for designing:

- Menu elements—menu titles, menu items, mnemonics, and so on
- Common menus—menus found in most applications
- Contextual menus—menus whose items affect the object or area under the pointer

To understand this chapter, you should be familiar with the menu-related terms (such as drop-down menu) in *Java Look and Feel Design Guidelines*, 2d ed. This chapter is intended only for applications with menus.

Menu Elements

Figure 22 shows menu elements in a typical application.

FIGURE 22   Menu Elements

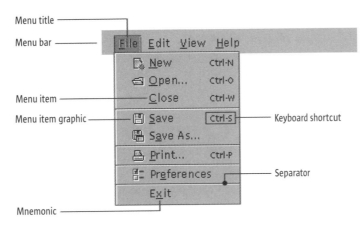

In Figure 22:

- Each menu title consists of exactly one word.

- The menu titles fit in a single line in the menu bar.

- The command name in each menu item is a single word or a short phrase, such as "Save As."

- No menu item has a command name identical to the menu's title. (For example, no item in the File menu is labeled "File.")

- All menu titles and menu items use headline capitalization style. (For more information about headline capitalization, see Chapter 4 of *Java Look and Feel Design Guidelines*, 2d ed.)

Menu elements in most applications should have these characteristics, each of which promotes usability.

When a window is at its default size, ensure that the titles of its drop-down menus all fit on a single line in the menu bar, without being truncated.

Ensure that the title of a drop-down menu consists of exactly one word.

In drop-down menus, ensure that the label of each menu item differs from the menu title.

Keyboard Shortcuts and Mnemonics for Menu Items   Keyboard shortcuts and mnemonics are keyboard equivalents to menu items.

- A **keyboard shortcut** is a keystroke combination (usually a modifier key and a character key, like Control-C) that activates a menu item from the keyboard, even if the relevant menu is not currently displayed.

- A **mnemonic** is an underlined alphanumeric character in a menu title or menu item. A mnemonic shows a user which key to press (sometimes in conjunction with the Alt key) to activate a menu item or navigate to it.

An item's mnemonic differs from its keyboard shortcut. Figure 22 on page 31 shows mnemonics and keyboard shortcuts for items in a typical File menu.

Table 5 lists mnemonics for typical menus and menu items. To use the mnemonics in Table 5, users can simultaneously press the Alt key and the character key that corresponds to the underlined letter or numeral. (For more information, see Chapter 6 of *Java Look and Feel Design Guidelines*, 2d ed.)

TABLE 5   Common Mnemonics

Menu Title	Menu Items
File	New, New Window, Open, Open in New Window, Open in Current Window, Close, Save, Save As, Page Setup, Print, Preferences, *File* Properties[1], Exit
Edit	Undo, Redo, Cut, Copy, Paste, Delete, Find, Find Again, Select All
Format	Bold, Italic, Underline, Align Left, Align Center, Align Right
View	Large Icons, Small Icons, List, Details, Sort By, Filter, Zoom In, Zoom Out, Refresh
Help	Contents, Tutorial, Index, Search, About *Application-Name*

1. Assign "e" as the mnemonic for the *File* Properties item only if the name represented by *File* contains no better letter for the mnemonic.

Table 6 lists common keyboard shortcuts.

TABLE 6   Common Keyboard Shortcuts

Sequence	Equivalent Menu Item
Ctrl-N	New (File menu)
Ctrl-O	Open (File menu)
Ctrl-W	Close (File menu)
Ctrl-S	Save (File menu)
Ctrl-P	Print (File menu)
Ctrl-Z	Undo (Edit menu)
Ctrl-Y	Redo (Edit menu)
Ctrl-X	Cut (Edit menu)
Ctrl-C	Copy (Edit menu)
Ctrl-V	Paste (Edit menu)
Delete	Delete (Edit menu)

TABLE 6   Common Keyboard Shortcuts *(Continued)*

Sequence	Equivalent Menu Item
Ctrl-F	Find (Edit menu)
Ctrl-G	Find Again (Edit menu)
Ctrl-H	Replace (Edit menu)
Ctrl-A	Select All (Edit menu)
Ctrl-B	Bold (Format menu)
Ctrl-I	Italic (Format menu)
Ctrl-U	Underline (Format menu)
Ctrl-J	Justify (Format menu)
Ctrl-L	Align Left (Format menu)
Ctrl-E	Align Center (Format menu)
Ctrl-R	Align Right (Format menu)
F1	Help
Shift-F1	Contextual help
F10	Refresh

For more information about keyboard shortcuts and mnemonics, see those topics in Chapter 6 of *Java Look and Feel Design Guidelines*, 2d ed. and elsewhere in that book.

☕ Assign mnemonics to all menu titles and menu items. Use the mnemonics in Table 5 if your application includes any of the menu titles and menu items listed there.

☕ Provide keyboard shortcuts for frequently used menu items. Use the keyboard shortcuts in Table 6, if possible.

Available and Unavailable Items   A menu item is dimmed when its command is **unavailable.** In Figure 23, the Paste and Paste Special items are unavailable and, therefore, dimmed.

FIGURE 23   Menu with Unavailable Items

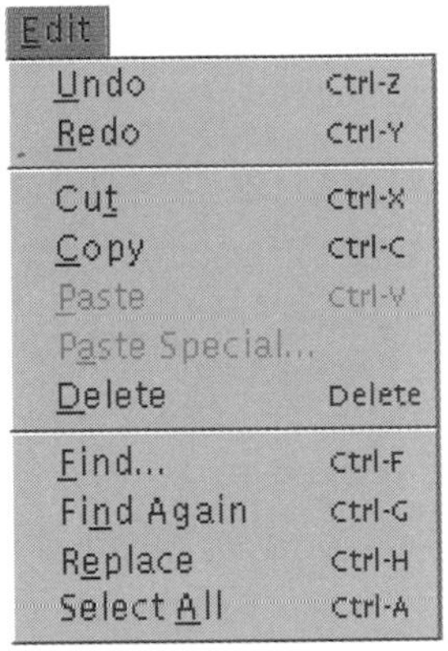

☕ Dim a menu item if it represents an unavailable command, and users can make that command available without exiting the application. If the command becomes available, undim the menu item. (For more information on available and unavailable menu items, see Chapter 9 of *Java Look and Feel Design Guidelines*, 2d ed.)

Additional Conventions for Menu Items
Like the conventions described so far in this chapter, the following conventions help users to work with menus.

Separators   You can group menu items by inserting separators between groups. In Figure 23, the Undo and Redo items of the Edit menu are a group, set apart from the menu's other groups by a separator.

Ellipses   An ellipsis (...) at the end of a menu item indicates that an application needs additional user input to execute the item's command. An ellipsis indicates that the application will display a dialog box before executing the command. However, not all menu items that open additional windows should have an ellipsis. For example, the About item in a Help menu should not end in an ellipsis.

☕ Place an ellipsis (...) at the end of a menu item only if that item opens a dialog box that requests user input for completing an action.

☕ Do not place an ellipsis (...) after a menu item that opens a property window.

Menu Item Graphics You can place graphics before the leading edge of menu items, as in Figure 22 on page 31.

Provide menu item graphics only if there are corresponding toolbar button graphics in your application. The graphics help users associate the toolbar button with the corresponding menu command. Provide menu item graphics for all the qualified menu items or for none of them.

The recommended menu graphics are at the following web site: `http://developer.java.sun.com/developer/techDocs/hi/repository/`

Common Menus

Common menus refers to the drop-down menus that are in most menu-driven applications. The common menus are:

- File menu
- Edit menu
- View menu
- Help menu

Figure 24 shows the common menus and their usual menu items.

FIGURE 24 Common Menus

Use the common menus and usual menu items as a starting point when designing menus.

In your application, provide a File menu and a Help menu. (You can change the title of the File menu, as discussed in "Typical File Menu" on page 37.) The other common menus are optional. When designing menus, include the optional common menus only if your application needs them. Similarly, within each menu, include optional items only if they fit your application's needs. Later sections of this chapter explain which menu items are required in each common menu and under which conditions they are required.

☕ In applications with drop-down menus, include a File menu and a Help menu in each application window. (You can rename the File menu, as explained in the next section.)

☕ When placing common menus in a menu bar, place them in this order: File, Edit, View, Help. Place any additional menus between the Edit menu and the View menu, or between the View menu and the Help menu.

Typical File Menu
An application's leftmost menu, typically titled "File," contains the following types of menu items:

- Items that affect a window's top-level object type—the type of object that the window represents, such as a file, mailbox, or computer.

- Items that affect the entire application—for example, application preferences.

- Items by which users interact with external resources. For example, in Figure 25, the Print menu item enables users to interact with a printer.

FIGURE 25   Example File Menu

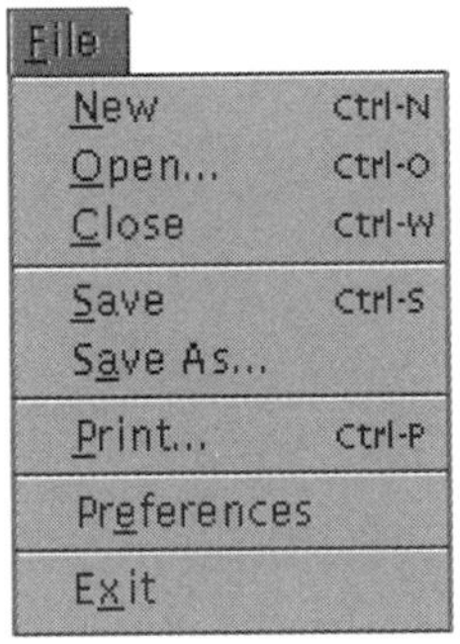

```
File
  New        Ctrl-N
  Open...     Ctrl-O
  Close       Ctrl-W

  Save        Ctrl-S
  Save As...

  Print...    Ctrl-P

  Preferences

  Exit
```

Although the title of the leftmost menu is usually "File," you can instead name it after the window's top-level object type—for example, "Console," "Mailbox," or "Computer."

NOTE – Except where noted, this chapter refers to an application's leftmost menu as the "*File* menu," though the menu's actual title might differ.

Place a menu item in the *File* menu if that item enables users to interact with an external resource, such as a printer.

☕ Ensure that the *File* menu is always the leftmost menu of the menu bar. In addition, ensure that the *File* menu's title is either "File" or the name of the object type that the window represents.

New Item   The New item, shown in Figure 26, enables users to create an object of the type that the window represents. (In contrast, the Open item, described on page 39, reopens an existing object of that type.)

FIGURE 26   New Menu Item

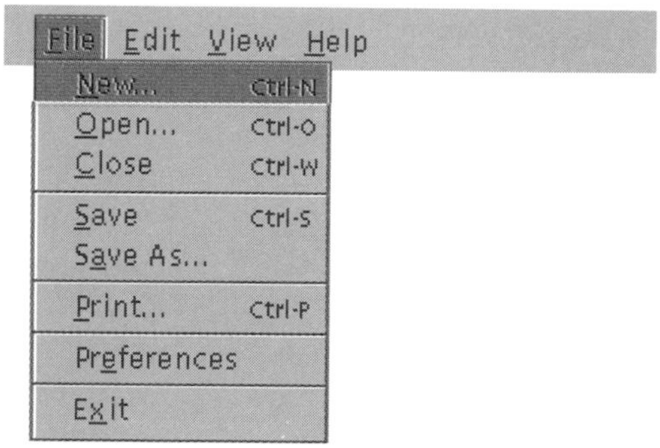

The New item has several variants, each for a different type of application. Some frequently used variants are:

- New…—Displays a dialog box.
- New (with a submenu indicator)—Opens a submenu, as in Figure 27.
- New *File*—Creates an object of type *File*.
- New Window—Creates a new primary window displaying, typically, a new view of the same objects that the current primary window displays.

FIGURE 27   New Menu Item with Submenu

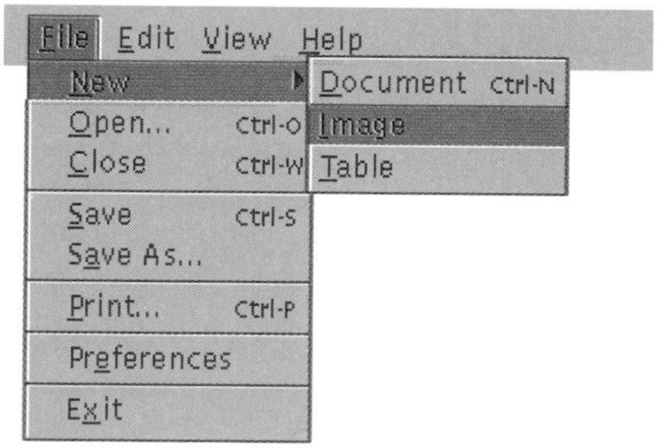

To determine which variant of the New item to use, decide whether your application will enable users to create objects in the current primary window, in a new primary window, or in either. A task analysis can help you make this decision. (To learn about task analysis, see a book such as *User and Task*

Analysis for Interface Design, described in "Related Books" on page xiv.) "Window Management and the File Menu" on page 49 can also help you decide which variant of the New item fits your application.

If users can create more than one type of object, the *File* menu can list more than one variant of the New item. For example, the *File* menu might list a New Mailbox item and a New Message item. If users can create ten or more types of objects, consider using a New… menu item to display a dialog box where users can choose a type of object.

☕ Include the New item in a window's *File* menu if users can create objects in that window.

☕ If users can create at least three types of objects—but fewer than ten types—ensure that the *File* menu's New item activates a submenu showing the types of objects that users can create.

☕ In a *File* menu, ensure that the New item (or any one of its variants, New…, New *File*, or New *File*…) creates an object either in the current primary window or in a new primary window.

☕ In a *File* menu, ensure that the New Window item (if present) creates a primary window—typically one containing a new view of the same objects displayed in the current primary window. If a menu item behaves in this way, label it New Window.

☕ If users can set parameters of a new object, include a New… or New *File*… item in the *File* menu. Display a dialog box to help users set the new object's parameters before the application creates the object. For example, an email application might display a dialog box to let users name a mailbox before the application creates it.

☕ In the *File* menu, if the New item has a submenu, assign the keyboard shortcut Ctrl-N to the most frequently used submenu item.

Open Item The Open item opens an existing object in the current primary window or a new primary window. Typically, users choose the object in a dialog box for choosing files or other objects.

The Open item has the following variants:

- Open (with a submenu indicator)
- Open… (displays a dialog box)
- Open in Current Window
- Open in Current Window…
- Open in New Window
- Open in New Window…

The correct form to use in your application depends on whether the application can open objects in:

- The current primary window
- A new primary window
- Either the current primary window or a new primary window

For help in deciding which variant of the Open item fits your application, see "Window Management and the File Menu" on page 49.

A *File* menu's New and Open items must manage windows in the same way. For example, if the New item creates objects in the current window, the Open item must also create objects in the current window.

☕ If users can open at least three types of objects—but fewer than ten types—ensure that the *File* menu's Open item activates a submenu showing the types of objects that users can open.

☕ In a *File* menu, if the Open item has a submenu, assign the keyboard shortcut Ctrl-O to the most frequently used submenu item.

☕ If your application needs a dialog box for choosing files, use the file-chooser dialog box in the Swing API of the Java Foundation Classes.

Close Item   The Close item closes the current primary window. Include the Close item only if your application can display more than one primary window. Group the Close item with the New item and the Open item.

☕ If your application supports more than one primary window, ensure that each *File* menu includes a Close menu item.

☕ In a *File* menu, ensure that the Close item closes an application's current primary window and only that window.

☕ If only one primary window remains open, ensure that the *File* menu's Close item behaves like that menu's Exit item. (For a description of the Exit item, see "Exit Item" on page 42.)

☕ If closing a window will discard a user's unsaved changes, warn the user by displaying an alert box.

Print Item   The Print item prints the current object. The Print item ends in an ellipsis if it will display a Print Options dialog box. Display a Print Options dialog box if users can set print options.

☕ If your application needs a Print Options dialog box, use the print-chooser dialog box in the Swing API of the JFC (Java Foundation Classes).

Preferences Item   The Preferences item displays a property sheet that lists preference settings for an entire application.

☕ If your application's users can set preferences, include a Preferences item in the *File* menu.

File Properties Item   The *File* Properties item sets properties of the application window's top-level object (for example, a mailbox).

☕ If a window's leftmost menu is named for the window's top-level object type (referred to here as *File*), and that object type has properties that users can display, ensure that the *File* menu includes an item labeled *File* Properties.

Most Recently Used (MRU) Menu List   Many applications provide a Most Recently Used (MRU) list so that users can reopen objects. The MRU list is a dynamic list of a user's most recently opened objects. The first object on the list is the one most recently used. If your application has an MRU list, assign mnemonics to the MRU numbers in the list, as shown in Figure 28.

FIGURE 28   Most Recently Used (MRU) List in a File Menu

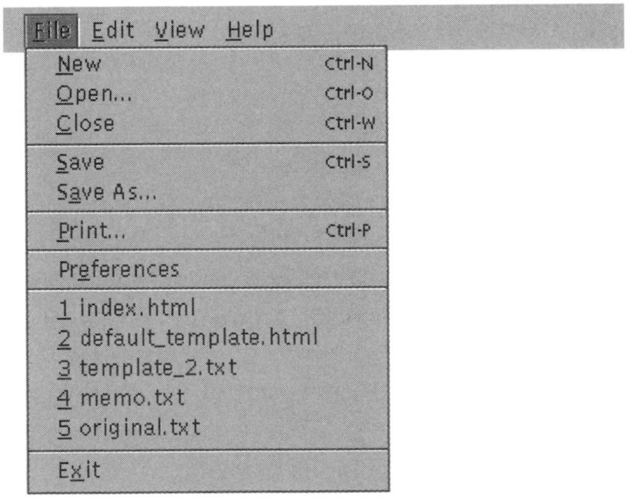

☕ If a *File* menu has a Most Recently Used list, place that list just above the menu's Exit item. Place one separator above the list and another separator below the list.

☕ If a *File* menu has a Most Recently Used list, ensure that the list displays no more than 10 objects.

Exit Item   The Exit item terminates an application, closing all its windows—no matter how many primary windows are open. In applications that can display multiple primary windows, the File menu includes an Exit item and a Close item. The Close item closes only the current primary window and then terminates the application if no other primary window is open. If just one primary window is open, the Exit item and the Close item have the same effect. (For more information on the Close item, see page 40.)

In applications that can display only a single primary window, the Exit item is the only way to close that window from the File menu. In such applications, the File menu does not include a Close item.

☕ Ensure that the Exit item is the final item in the *File* menu.

☕ Ensure that the Exit item closes all associated windows and terminates the application.

☕ If terminating the application will discard a user's unsaved changes, warn the user by displaying an alert box.

Typical Edit Menu   The Edit menu contains items with which users can modify an application's objects. Some of the menu's items, such as the Find item, work on the current window. Others, such as the Delete item, work on currently selected objects. Figure 29 shows an example of an Edit menu.

FIGURE 29   Example Edit Menu

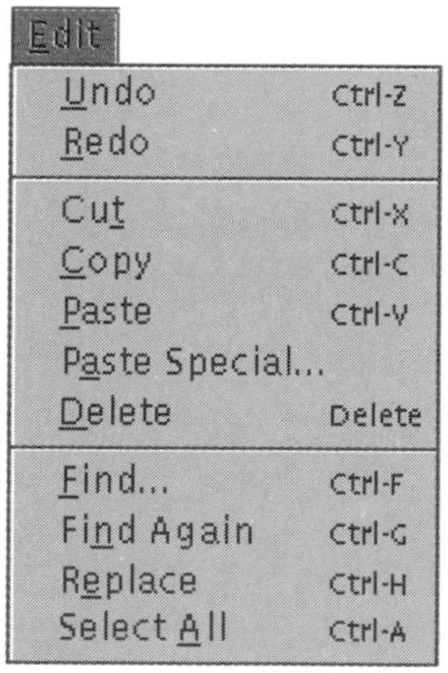

Updating Labels of Menu Items   In the Edit menu, you can continuously update the labels of some items to reflect your application's state or the object type on which the menu item operates. For example, you could continuously update an Undo *CommandName* item—where *CommandName* changes to the name of the most recent command, such as Undo Paste. Continuous updating is useful for labeling Delete menu items, where the label can reflect the type of object that will be deleted—for example, Delete Group or Delete Alias.

Paste Special Item   The Edit menu can include a Paste Special item that enables users to control the format of pasted data. Optionally, this menu item can display a submenu or dialog box from which users can choose one of the formats in which data can be pasted. For example, text might be pasted as formatted text or as unformatted text.

Properties Item   Many applications include a Properties item in the Edit menu. The Properties item always works on the current selection. If no objects are selected, the Properties item should be unavailable and dimmed. Putting a Properties item in the Edit menu is appropriate if the application has no *Object* menu or when the application has more than one *Object* menu. (For more information about *Object* menus, see "Additional Menus" on page 45.)

A Properties item in the Edit menu differs from a *File* Properties item in the *File* menu. A *File* Properties item sets properties of a window's top-level object (for example, a word-processing document open in that window). In contrast, a Properties item in the Edit menu sets the properties of an object that can be selected in a window (for example, a table in an open word-processing document).

☕ If your application has an Edit menu, place it second on the menu bar, directly to the right of the *File* menu.

☕ Continuously update the labels of items in the Edit menu so that the labels indicate the object type on which the items act.

☕ If you include an Undo item in the Edit menu, also include a Redo item in that menu. Never use an Undo item to enable users to redo a command.

☕ If users can paste data from the clipboard in different formats, include a Paste Special item in the Edit menu. The Paste Special item should perform an operation, display a submenu, or display a dialog box listing paste options. If the item performs an operation, label the item Paste *Format* instead of Paste Special. Replace *Format* with a word that suggests the format in which data will be pasted—for example, Paste Unformatted or Paste Formula.

 If the Edit menu includes a Properties item, place that item last in the menu and precede it with a separator.

 When adding application-specific items to the Edit menu, place them after the group of more typical items to which they relate most closely. (For example, if your application has a Paste Special item, place it after the Paste item, as in Figure 29.) Alternatively, place the application-specific items at the end of the Edit menu, but before the Properties item (if there is one).

Typical View Menu

Many applications include a View menu, whose menu items alter the presentation of data. For example, the View menu of some applications include items such as Large Icons, Small Icons, List, and Details. Figure 30 shows an example of a View menu.

FIGURE 30   Example View Menu

The appropriate items for the View menu depend on which objects your application contains. For example, the View menu of a network management application might include:

■ A List item—to display a network's computers as a list
■ A Topology item—to display the same network's computers as a topological graph

 Ensure that items in the View menu change only the presentation of data in the current primary window. Ensure that the items do not change the data itself.

 In the View menu, indicate which view the window currently displays. To do so, place a radio button next to each item for choosing a particular view (as shown in Figure 30). (For information about radio button menu items, see Chapter 9 of *Java Look and Feel Design Guidelines*, 2d ed.)

Typical Help Menu
The Help menu enables users to open an application's online help system. In addition, the Help menu provides access to the About box, which displays information about the copyright, license, and version of the application. (For more information about the Help menu, see Chapter 9 of *Java Look and Feel Design Guidelines*, 2d ed.)

FIGURE 31   Example Help Menu

☕ In a Help menu, place the About *Application-name* item last, and precede it with a separator.

Additional Menus
When designing menus, use the common menus (described on page 36) as a starting point. Your application might, however, need more menus if it has more items than the common menus can display. When adding menus beyond the common ones, start by adding a menu for the primary object types in the application window. This chapter refers to such menus as *Object* menus.

Object Menus
Object menus contain menu items for creating, deleting, and modifying objects of the type *Object*. *Object* refers to an object type within the window's top-level object type, referred to here as *File*. An *Object* menu differs from a renamed *File* menu. (For information on *File* and renaming the *File* menu, see page 37.)

Figure 32 shows examples of *Object* menus.

FIGURE 32   Example Object Menus

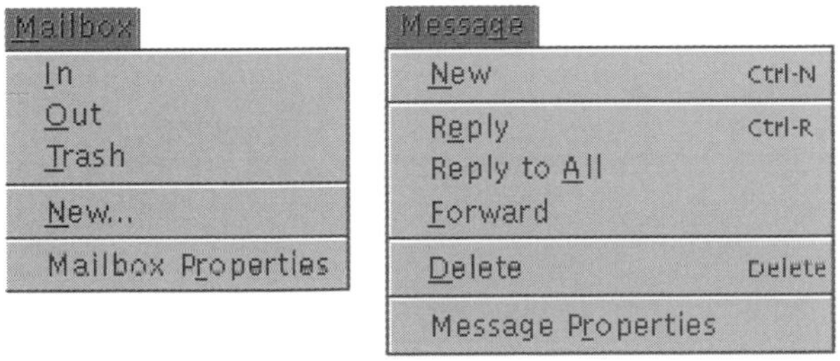

When including an *Object* menu in your application, place the New, Open, and Save items for that object type in its *Object* menu, not in the *File* menu. For example, an email application might define two *Object* menus labeled Mailbox and Message. The Mailbox menu would include items for creating and modifying mailboxes. The Message menu would include items for creating and modifying mail messages.

Avoid creating too many *Object* menus. Decide which objects should be prominent in your user interface and which ones are subordinate to other objects. Most subordinate objects should not have their own menu. If a menu item relates to a subordinate object, you can place that item in a menu associated with the superior object. For example, if a window contains a table, you can place table-related menu items (such as Delete Row) on the window's Edit menu.

For guidelines about the correct order of menus in the menu bar, see "Common Menus" on page 36.

☕ When you include an *Object* menu, place the New, Open, and Save menu items for that object type in that *Object* menu.

☕ Use specific labels for your *Object* menus. Do not use generic *Object* menus labeled either "Object" or "Selected."

Object Menus and the Action Menu
If your application has no maximum number of top-level object types, you cannot create an *Object* menu for each top-level object type. Consider including an Action menu instead of an *Object* menu.

An Action menu is a menu whose title is "Action" and whose contents vary depending on the application's context and the current selection. Also consider including an Action menu if you expect your application's top-level object type to change.

For example, an application consisting of two tools could load one set of menu items in its Action menu when one tool was in current use, but load another set of menu items when the other tool was in use. Each set of menu items would be specific to the current tool.

In rare situations you might need *Object* menus as well as an Action menu — *Object* menus for a few top-level objects used widely in your application and an Action menu for other object-based menu items.

☕ Provide an Action menu under either of the following conditions:

- Your application has no maximum number of top-level object types.
- The top-level object types can vary widely.

☕ When providing an Action menu, place it directly to the left of the View menu.

☕ If you provide an Action menu, make the contents of the Action menu dependent on your application's context and current selection.

Beyond Object Menus and the Action Menu   After you evaluate the common menus and, optionally, add *Object* menus or an Action menu, you might still need more menus. Typically, the titles of such additional menus are verbs — for example, "Insert," "Compose," or "Debug." The items in these menus should relate to a task that users perform frequently.

☕ If you application has additional menus, place them directly to the right of the *Object* menus — if there are any — and directly to the left of the Help menu.

Contextual Menus
A **contextual menu** is a menu displayed when a user presses **mouse button 2** while the pointer is over an object or area associated with that menu. Contextual menus are one of two main types of menus — the other type being drop-down menus, which users choose from a menu bar. Figure 33 shows a contextual menu.

FIGURE 33   Contextual Menu (Displayed Over a Table)

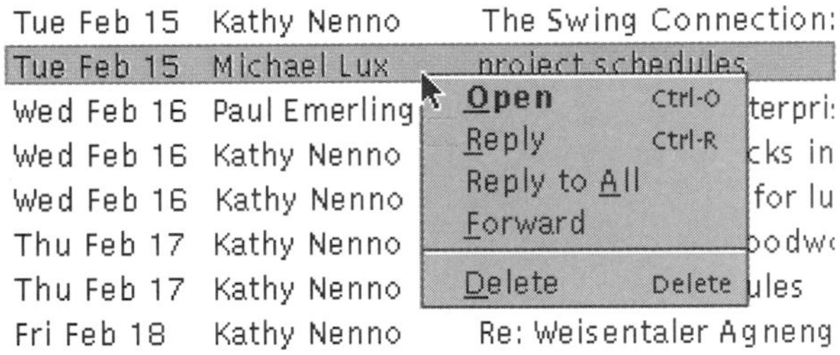

Contextual menus provide quick access to menu items available elsewhere in an application. A contextual menu should include only frequently used menu items; otherwise, it will be hard to use.

Although contextual menus and drop-down menus are alike in most ways, contextual menus differ from drop-down menus in the following ways:

- Contextual menus are displayed only when a user presses mouse button 2 or Shift-F10.

- Contextual menus are composed of:
  - Menu items that affect the object or selection under the pointer

- Menu items for the entire window
- Menu items that do not require a selection

The correct menu items for a contextual menu depend on where the pointer is when a user opens that menu. Table 7 describes the correct types of menu items for contextual menus opened from various pointer positions.

TABLE 7   Correct Menu Items for Contextual Menus

Pointer Position When Menu Opens	Correct Menu Items
Not on an object or selection	• Items that do not require a selection • Items that apply to the entire window
On a single object that is not selected	• Items that operate on the object under the pointer • Items that do not require a selection • Items that apply to the entire window
On a selection	• Items that can operate each object in the selection (an intersection, not a union) • Items that do not require a selection • Items that apply to the entire window

If a user opens a contextual menu for an object that is not selected, that object becomes selected. The new selection cancels any previous selection.

Some objects have a **default command**, executed if a user double-clicks the object. When displaying the contextual menu for such an object, use bold to display the menu item that activates the default command. For an example, see Figure 33, in which Open is the default command.

The following guidelines help you design contextual menus. These guidelines supplement those in Chapter 9 of *Java Look and Feel Design Guidelines*, 2d ed.

☕ Each item in a contextual menu must be available elsewhere in your application. Provide contextual menus only as conveniences that are redundant with other controls—typically with items in your application's drop-down menus.

☕ If your application has contextual menus, ensure that it has them for all its objects.

☕ Include only frequently used menu items in contextual menus.

☕ If the object of a contextual menu has a default command, place that command at the top of the contextual menu. In addition, display the command in bold.

☕ Do not display unavailable menu items that cannot apply to the current object. In an open contextual menu, dim unavailable menu items that can apply to the current object.

☕ In a contextual menu for a selection, ensure that each menu item that operates on an object can be applied to each object in the selection. (That is, ensure that the set of menu items for the selected objects is an intersection, not a union.)

☕ When designing contextual menus, follow the rules in Table 7 on page 48.

Window Management and the File Menu

The correct design for an application's *File* menu depends on how the application manages windows that display top-level objects. A window's top-level object is the object that the window represents—such as a file, mailbox, or computer.

In most applications, users create top-level objects or open them by choosing the New item or Open item from the *File* menu. Some applications have one or more variants of these menu items—for example, New, New…, New *Object*, or New Window.

To determine whether your application's *File* menu needs one or more of these variants, you need to decide how the application will manage windows that display top-level objects. For example, your application might either:

- Open a new window for each top-level object
- Reuse a single window for all top-level objects

This section helps you decide which menu items to include for creating and opening top-level objects. The section is based on several example *File* menus, each for a different type of window management.

For general information and guidelines about the *File* menu, see "Typical File Menu" on page 37.

When Window Reuse Is the Default   This section provides examples of window-management styles that, by default, open and create objects in the primary window from which a user has chosen the New or Open menu item. For examples of styles in which the default action is to open a new window, see "When Opening a New Window Is the Default" on page 51.

Using a Single Primary Window   Figure 34 shows the *File* menu of an application with only one primary window. The *File* menu's New and Open menu items always reuse that primary window.

FIGURE 34   File Menu for an Application's Only Primary Window

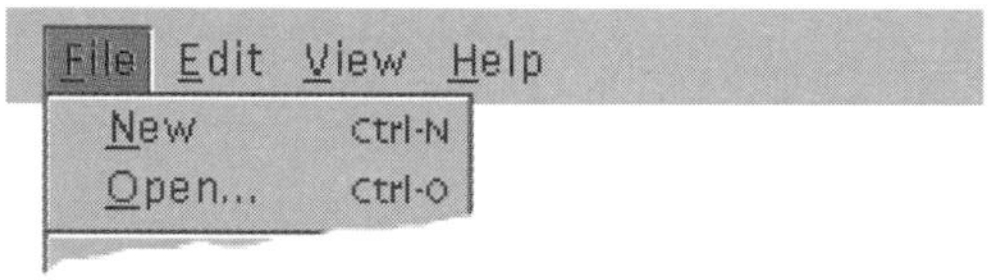

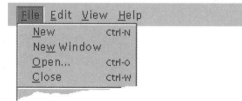

Typically, such a *File* menu is suitable only for simple applications whose users need to view only one object at a time.

Reusing the Current Window and Creating Windows   In Figure 35, the New and Open items always display objects in the current primary window. To create more primary windows, users can choose the New Window item. Typically, an application's New Window item displays the same contents as the window from which it was created. Alternatively, the New Window item can open a primary window containing nothing or a newly created object.

FIGURE 35   File Menu for Reusing the Current Window and Creating Windows

The *File* menu in Figure 35 is suitable for applications that display one object at a time, but whose users sometimes need to view two or more objects at the same time—each object in its own primary window. For example, a user might need to compare two documents.

In Figure 35, opening an object in a new window requires that users choose two *File* menu items, in order—the New Window item followed by the Open item. Design a *File* menu like the one in Figure 35 only if a task analysis has shown that users rarely need to open an object in a new window. (To learn about task analysis, see a book such as *User and Task Analysis for Interface Design*, described in "Related Books" on page xiv.)

Reusing the Current Window and Opening Objects in New Windows   In Figure 36, the *File* menu enables users to open an object in the current primary window or in a new primary window. The *File* menu's Open item reuses the current primary window. The Open in New Window item opens an object in a new primary window.

FIGURE 36   File Menu to Reuse the Current Window and Create New Windows

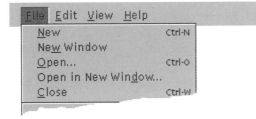

The *File* menu in Figure 36 is appropriate only if a task analysis has shown both that:

- The application's users need an Open menu item and an Open in New Window item—for example, to compare two objects by displaying one in the current primary window and the other in a new primary window.

- Most of the users prefer to open an object in the current primary window.

In Figure 36, the New Window menu item always creates an object in a new primary window.

When Opening a New Window Is the Default   This section illustrates window-management styles where the default action is to open a new window for each newly created object or newly opened object.

Placing All Objects in Separate Primary Windows   In Figure 37, the New and Open items always create a primary window.

FIGURE 37   File Menu for Placing All Objects in Separate Windows

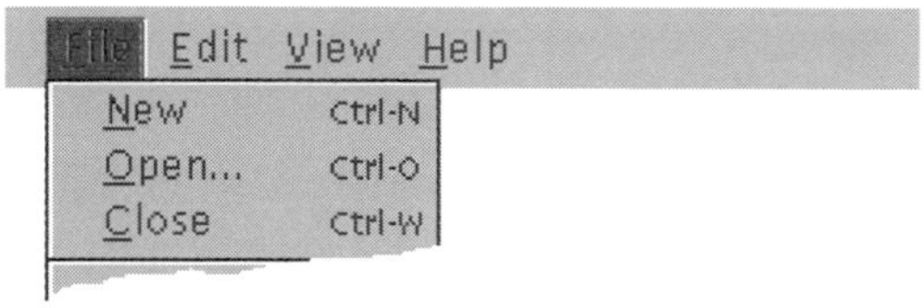

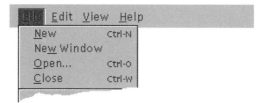

The *File* menu in Figure 37 is appropriate only if users often keep two or more objects open at the same time. Such menus require a Close item because more than one primary window can be open at the same time.

Displaying Objects in Separate Windows with Duplicate Window Operation   The *File* menu in Figure 38 displays each new object in a new primary window. The *File* menu includes a New Window item as a shortcut for creating a copy of the current object. The New Window item always displays the same view of the object as the window from which it was created.

FIGURE 38   File Menu to Display Objects in Separate Windows with Duplicate
                    Window Operation

In Figure 38, the *File* menu is identical to the one in Figure 35. The New menu item and the Open menu item, however, behave differently in each menu. If you have correctly matched the behavior of the menu items to the users' tasks, users will notice no inconsistency between applications after using the menu items a few times.

Displaying Objects in Separate Windows and Allowing Current Window Reuse   In the *File* menu shown in Figure 39, the New and Open items create primary windows.

FIGURE 39   File Menu to Display Objects in Separate Windows and Permit Current Window Reuse

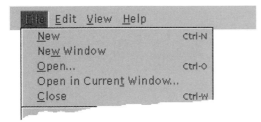

The Open in Current Window item supports tasks where users do not want to create an additional window. An application's New Window menu item can show the same object as the window from which it was activated, or it can show an empty window, depending on which operation users will perform more often.

Each of the designs described in this section is suited to a different situation. To determine which design is appropriate for your application, perform a task analysis.

4: BEHAVIOR

Behavior refers to how applications interact with users. *Java Look and Feel Design Guidelines*, 2d ed. discusses that topic. This chapter provides additional information about the following aspects of behavior:

- Modes
- Selecting multiple objects
- Filtering and searching
- Tool tips

Modes

In some applications, the effects of a user's actions differ in different situations, or **modes**, defined in the application. Often, a mode lets users perform only certain actions. For example, in one mode of a drawing application, clicking one object after another might select those objects. In a different mode of the same application, clicking one object after another might draw a line between those objects. In other words, the same action would have a different effect in different modes.

By limiting users' potential actions, modes make it easier for software developers to translate those actions into code. Applications with modes can be hard to use because:

- Users must remember which mode is in effect. If users are unaware of modes or forget to change modes, the users' actions have incorrect effects.
- Users must switch between modes, which requires extra mouse actions or extra keystrokes.

Sometimes, modes can help users, typically by preventing users from accidentally performing unwanted actions—for example, activating a command button in a graphical user interface while trying to lay out the interface.

☕ Avoid defining modes in your application, especially if users are likely to be hurried, as when responding to alarms.

Modal Secondary Windows   A **modal secondary window** prevents users from interacting with other windows of an application until that modal window is closed. (In contrast, a **modeless secondary window** does not prevent users from interacting with that application.) Among the types of modal secondary windows are modal dialog boxes and modal alert boxes. Chapter 8 of *Java Look and Feel Design Guidelines*, 2d ed. describes modal and modeless dialog boxes as well as alert boxes, which can also be modal or modeless.

Modal secondary windows can make it harder for users to complete their current task. For example, a modal dialog box prevents users from copying information from outside that dialog box—even if the information is needed to complete fields of the dialog box.

Use modeless secondary windows whenever possible. If your application uses modal secondary windows, keep them in front of the application's other windows. (An application's users can override this behavior by setting preferences in the operating system.)

☕ Use a modal dialog box only if a user might put the application in an inconsistent state that the user cannot easily remedy. For example, a user might put the application in an inconsistent state by making changes in other windows while the dialog box is open.

☕ Use a modal alert box only to alert users of a condition that requires user input before the application can proceed. For example, create a modal alert box to verify that a user wants to perform an action that will have irreversible consequences.

Modes Set from Tool Palettes   Some applications, such as graphics applications, have **tool palettes**—internal utility windows whose buttons enable users to choose a tool, such as a paint brush, from a set of tools. Typically, each tool corresponds to a particular mode. Clicking a button in a tool palette changes the current mode and, as a result, changes the meaning of mouse operations—for example, causing each mouse click to insert an object instead of selecting one.

In tool palettes, a mode can stay in effect until a user performs the next action or until a user activates a different mode.

☕ If a user chooses a tool from a tool palette, causing a different mode to take effect, change the pointer's shape to indicate which tool and mode are in effect. For as long as that tool's mode is in effect, visually emphasize the tool's button in the palette by displaying it with the pressed appearance. (For information about command buttons with the pressed, available, or unavailable appearance, see Chapter 10 in *Java Look and Feel Design Guidelines*, 2d ed.)

Application-Wide Modes

Some applications have **application-wide modes**, which change the effect of users' actions throughout the application. An example of an application-wide mode is the Edit mode or Run mode of a typical GUI builder. The same mouse actions that modify controls in Edit mode activate controls in Run mode. For example, clicking a Print button in Edit mode would select that button so that the user could resize or otherwise modify it. Clicking the same Print button in Run mode would issue a command to print a document.

☕ If your application has application-wide modes, provide more than one way for users to change from one to another. Examples of ways to change between application-wide modes include menu items, command buttons, and keyboard shortcuts. By providing more than one way to change between modes, you make the modes more accessible.

☕ If your application has application-wide modes, provide visible cues so that users know which mode is in effect. For example, in a GUI-building application with an Edit mode and a Run mode, you might display a grid background only in Edit mode so that users could distinguish it from Run mode.

Selecting Multiple Objects

Users sometimes want to use a single command to perform the same action on multiple objects—that is, on more than one object at a time. To provide this capability in your application, you first need to provide multiple selection, the ability to select more than one object at a time.

Follow these rules when enabling users to select multiple objects:

- When multiple objects are selected, each command that can apply only to a single object is unavailable—for example, a command that renames an object.

- Clicking an object (with the primary mouse button) deselects any existing selection and selects the object. An alternative is to press the spacebar while keyboard focus is on an object. (For information on mouse operations, see Chapter 6 of *Java Look and Feel Design Guidelines*, 2d ed.)

- Shift-clicking an object extends the selection from the most recently selected object to the object under the pointer. An alternative is pressing Shift-spacebar while keyboard focus is on the object.
- Control-clicking an object toggles its selection without affecting the selection of any other objects. This operation can result in selecting more than one range of objects. An alternative is pressing Control-spacebar while keyboard focus is on an object.
- Dragging—moving the mouse while pressing a mouse button—selects the objects inside the **bounding box**. (Dragging works this way only in a 2-dimensional selection area, such as an **icon pane**.)

For more information about multiple selection in lists and in tables, see "Selection Models and Editing Models for Tables" on page 66. In addition, see Chapter 12 and Appendix A of *Java Look and Feel Design Guidelines*, 2d ed.

☕ Enable users to select multiple objects in a component if any of the component's commands can apply to more than one object at time.

☕ If users can select multiple objects with the mouse, enable users to select multiple objects with the keyboard as well.

☕ When users use the mouse to select multiple objects, select each object whose center is within the bounding box.

Filtering and Searching a Set of Objects

When working with a large set of objects, users sometimes want to view only objects with particular properties. For example, a user of an email application might want to see only message headers representing unread messages. **Searching** and **filtering** are application features that let a user specify which objects a window should display, based on the user's criteria. A user's criteria are called a filter (in filtering) or a query (in searching).

- Filtering starts from a window displaying a full set of objects, and then omits from the window all objects except those that match the filter.
- Searching starts from an empty window, and then displays only objects that match the query. (This does not apply to types of searching that select objects from a set of objects currently displayed in a window.)

Providing filtering and searching can improve an application's scalability.

NOTE – Sorting a set of objects can be an easier way to provide most of the benefits of filtering the set. For information on sorting, see "Row Sorting" on page 80. In addition, see Chapter 12 of *Java Look and Feel Design Guidelines*, 2d ed.

You can provide two kinds of filtering and searching in your application:

- Complex filtering and searching—Users use a dialog box to specify a filter or query, which can specify any property or set of properties.
- Simple filtering and searching—Users manipulate a visible control (such as a list or menu) to choose from a set of previously defined filters or queries.

Complex Filtering and Searching

When providing complex filtering or complex searching, follow these guidelines.

☕ Provide a filter or query for a set of objects if users cannot view the entire set without scrolling it.

☕ Unless your application takes less than four seconds to start displaying the complete results of a filter or search, display the results a portion at a time.

☕ Provide an easy way for users to execute a query or filter again after new data becomes available.

☕ Enable users to name, save, reuse, and modify custom filters and queries.

☕ Enable users to construct a single request from multiple filter terms or multiple query terms.

☕ If the data displayed in a window is the result of a filter or query, indicate that fact above the data. If possible, indicate which filter or query was used to obtain the data.

Simple Filtering and Searching

If users will use certain filters or queries repeatedly, provide quick access to those filters or queries through visible controls. Filters and queries accessible in this way are called simple filters and simple queries.

To enable users to choose simple filters, you can place menu items on the View menu or in a combo box, as in Figure 40.

FIGURE 40 Simple Filters

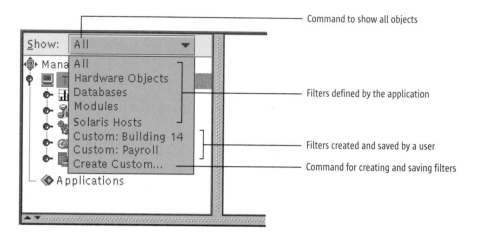

In Figure 40, the combo box includes the following items:

- A command to show all objects
- A set of simple filters defined by the application
- Simple filters that users have created, named, and saved
- A command to create and name a new filter

Filters can be more complex than the one in Figure 40. Figure 41 shows a more complex filter.

FIGURE 41   Complex Filter

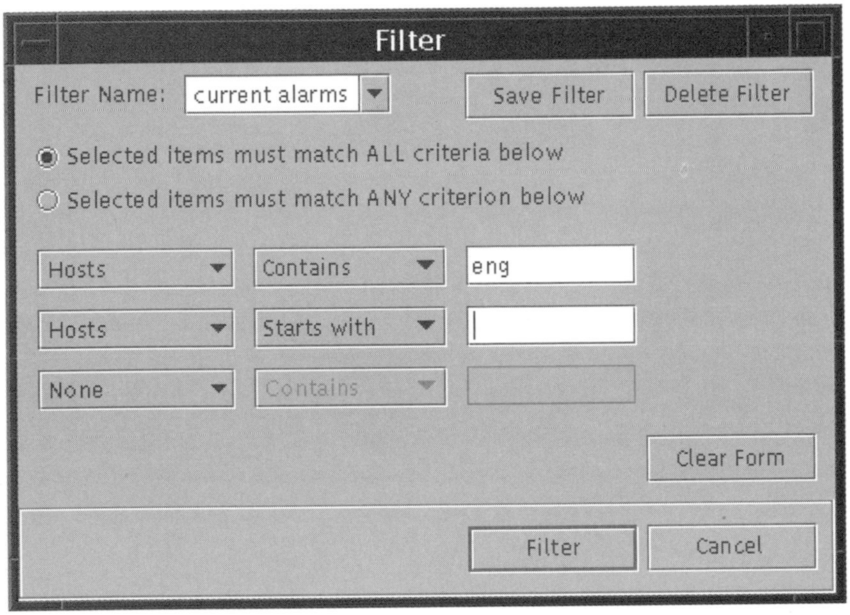

A task analysis can help you determine both:

- Whether simple filters and queries might be useful in your application, and
- Which types of filters and queries to provide

For references on task analysis, see "Related Books" on page xiv.

☕ Provide simple filters or simple queries if users need to refer to subsets of information repeatedly.

Stopping Searches and Filter Operations

Users sometimes need to stop a search or filter operation before it is complete—typically, because the operation is taking too long. Users should be able stop a search or filter operation at any time by clicking a command button that, typically, is labeled `Stop`, `Stop Search`, or `Stop Filtering`.

If a user stops a search or filter, your application should display a message stating that any displayed search results are incomplete.

☕ Indicate a stopped search or filter by placing a message outside the results but near where they are described—for example, in the title area of a table. Figure 42 shows a stopped search indicated by a message ("Stopped by User") displayed above the results. (For more information, see "Letting Users Stop Commands in Progress" on page 105.)

FIGURE 42   Stopped Search (Indicated by Text Above the Results)

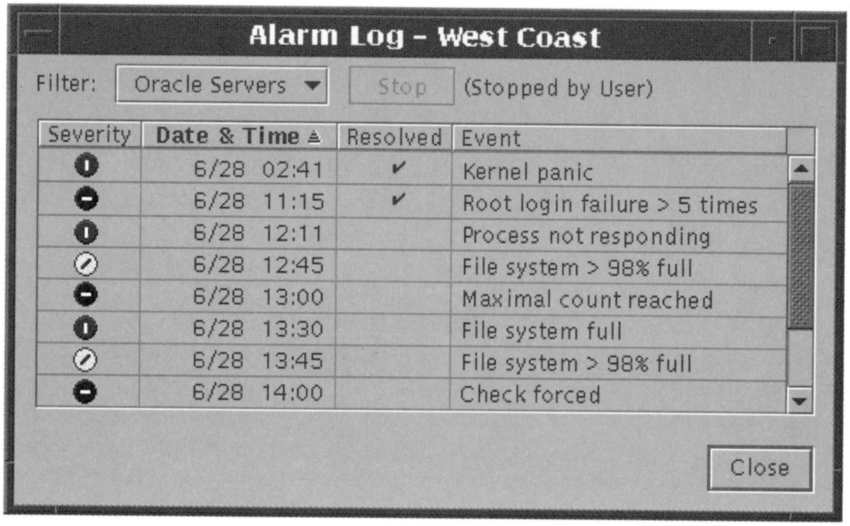

Tool Tips

Tool tips are small rectangles of text that describe a component or area whenever the pointer is over it. Among the properties of an application's tool tips are:

- **Onset delay**—the amount of time before a tool tip is displayed
- **Duration**—the amount of time for which a tool tip is displayed

An application's settings for the onset delay and duration of tool tips apply to all tool tips in the application.

Choosing an appropriate onset delay and duration for your application's tool tips improves their usability. This section provides guidelines that help you choose an appropriate onset delay and duration.

For additional guidelines about tool tips, see Chapter 9 of *Java Look and Feel Design Guidelines*, 2d ed.

Provide a tool tip for each control in your application.

Set the tool tip duration to at least 15 seconds if any tool tip is longer than 10 words or if any tool tip provides information, such as numerical data, that users need to analyze.

If either or both of the following statements are true, set the onset delay of your application's tool tips to no more than 250 milliseconds:

- At least one tool tip provides information that all users need.
- At least one tool tip displays data that users can find only in tool tips—for example, numerical values represented by bars in a bar graph.

If neither statement is true, consider using the JFC's default values for the onset delay and duration of tool tips.

5:   IDIOMS

One main characteristic of a well-designed user interface is consistency among its parts. This characteristic helps users learn similar parts of the user interface faster. You can help users learn your application's user interface faster by creating its similar parts from the same sets of JFC components— that is, by implementing the same patterns, or **idioms**.

This chapter explains what idioms are and then describes idioms for:

- Selecting and editing in tables provided by your application
- Arranging such tables
- Combining a tree component with a table
- Working with text fields and lists
- Displaying a hierarchy of containers in a split pane

Overview of Idioms

In user interfaces, an idiom is a set of components configured in a standardized way to provide a particular appearance and behavior. Just as idioms in a spoken language (such as "giving up" in English) have a meaning that cannot be derived from that of their individual words, idioms in the Java look and feel have usefulness that cannot be derived from that of their individual JFC components.

If you provide idioms consistently throughout your application, users come to recognize each idiom, even in new contexts, and can correctly infer what each idiom enables them to do.

An example of a widely used idiom is the **Browse idiom**, shown in Figure 43.

FIGURE 43   Example of an Idiom (the Browse Idiom)

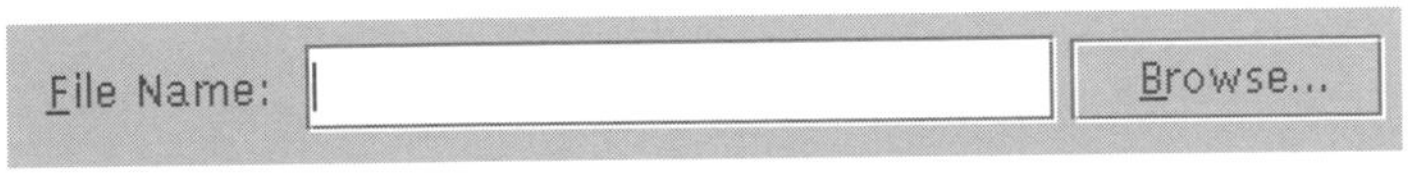

The Browse idiom enables users to type or choose the name of an existing object, such as a file. This idiom always consists of a label, an editable text field, and a command button. Each time users see the Browse idiom, they know that they can complete the text field by typing or by clicking the command button to choose text from a list. (The Browse idiom is described in detail on page 84.)

Although the JFC provides the components that make up idioms, your development team is responsible for implementing the idioms used in your application. This chapter describes idioms that you can use in the Java look and feel and provides guidelines to help your team implement each idiom.

Idioms for Selecting and Editing in Tables

If your application provides tables in which users can select and edit, you can make selecting and editing easier for users by consistently displaying the same idioms. This section describes:

- Concepts for selecting and editing in **application-provided tables**
- Idioms that enable users to select and edit in such tables

For information on table layout and order, see "Idioms for Arranging a Table" on page 75.

Selection Models and Editing Models for Tables

To enable users to select and edit in a table, you need to provide:

- A **selection model**—a set of rules and techniques for selecting a portion of the table, such as a cell or row
- An **editing model**—a set of rules and techniques for editing a portion of a table

This section provides guidelines to help you choose the correct selection model and editing model for your application's tables.

For an introduction to selection models for tables, see Chapter 12 of *Java Look and Feel Design Guidelines*, 2d ed. Of the selection models described in that chapter, use a **row-selection model** or a **cell-selection model**.

Row selection differs from cell selection in that selecting a cell also selects the entire row containing that cell. Tables using a row-selection model are called **row-selection tables**. Tables using a cell-selection model are called **cell-selection tables**.

The recommended types of row selection are:

- Single row
- Single range of rows
- Multiple distinct rows
- Multiple ranges of rows

The recommended types of cell selection are:

- Single cell
- Single range of cells

Choose the selection model that offers a table's users as much flexibility as they need.

☕ Use a row-selection model in tables where rows need to be operated on as a unit.

☕ In tables, enable users to select one or more ranges of rows or cells.

Using Row-Selection Models   You can use a row-selection table if users can operate on a row's contents only as a unit. For example, you can use a row-selection table if users need to update several interdependent cells at the same time — such as before committing a record to a database that verifies whether the interdependent values are consistent with one another.

You can associate commands with a row-selection table to enable users to manipulate its rows. Figure 44 shows a table with such commands, each represented as a command button to the right of the table.

FIGURE 44   Row-Selection Table with Associated Command Buttons

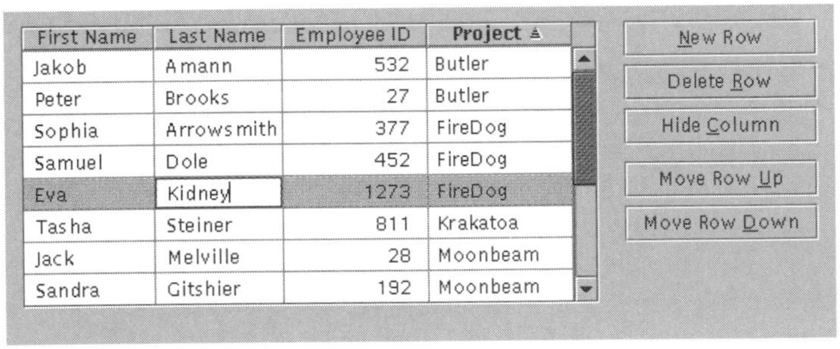

For a row-selection table, the correct set of commands depends on the table's editing model. Some commands can be used with any row-selection table, regardless of its editing model.

Table 11 describes those commands. For a list of commands and mnemonics for each editing model, see "Editing Row-Selection Tables" on page 69.

TABLE 8   Commands for Any Row-Selection Table

Command	Mnemonic	Description
New Row	N	Adds a new row directly above the uppermost row of the selected rows or, if there is no selection, adds a new row at the table's end. The New Row command selects the new row, deselecting any previous selection.
Delete Row	R	Deletes the selected rows.
Move Row Up	U	Moves the selected rows up by one row. If a user applies the Move Row Up command to a selection containing nonadjacent items, the command works as if the user performed it on each of the items separately. The items retain their positions relative to one another.
Move Row Down	D	Moves the selected rows down by one row. If a user applies the Move Row Down command to a selection containing nonadjacent items, the command works as if the user performed it on each of the items separately.

If you use the default names for commands that manipulate row-selection tables, assign the recommended mnemonics to those commands. (Table 8 lists the default names and the recommended mnemonics.)

In row-selection tables, command buttons for Move Row Up and Move Row Down can sometimes be labeled Move Up and Move Down, as in Figure 45. Use these short labels only if space is limited and if the purpose of each button is clear to users. If you use the short labels, use them for both buttons or for neither.

If a user deletes a row of a row-selection table, move the selection to a different row. Follow these rules:

- If the deleted row was the table's only row, either:
  - Display the table with a single empty row, which is selected, or
  - Display the table with no rows, if the user can add rows.

- If the deleted row was not the table's only row but was the table's bottom row, select the row directly above the deleted row.

- If the deleted row was neither the table's only row nor the bottom row, select the row directly below the deleted row.

Editing Row-Selection Tables   To enable users to edit in row-selection tables, you can use either the **external editing model** or the **internal editing model**. Tables using one of these models are called "externally editable" or "internally editable."

External Editing Model—In this model, users can edit a table row only by entering values in an **editing area**, located outside the table and, typically, just below it. The editing area includes editable text fields, combo boxes, or other editable components that enable users to type or choose input values. Each editable component in the editing area must correspond to a single column in the table.

Use the external editing model in row-selection tables if users can edit a row's contents only as a unit. For example, use the external editing model if, after users edits a row, your application must perform actions—such as a database update or a cell-interdependent validity check—that require the row's values to be consistent with one another.

Figure 45 shows a row-selection table that uses the external editing model.

FIGURE 45   Row-Selection Table with External Editing

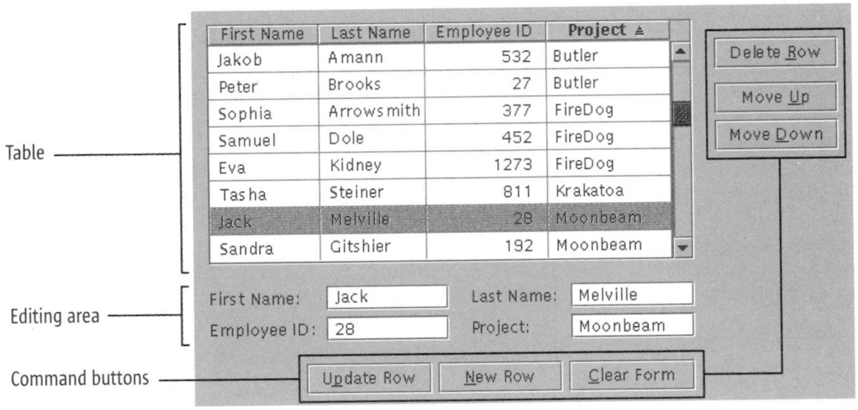

In Figure 45, the user has selected Jack Melville's row. Selecting a row updates the editing area's input fields with values from the table's uppermost selected row (in this example, only one row is selected). Selecting a row also makes the Update Row button and the New Row button available. (The Update Row button and the New Row button copy values from the editing area's input fields into the table itself. The copied values remain displayed in the input fields.)

If, in the editing area, the user edits the Project field, changing its value from `Moonbeam` to, for example, `Firedog`, the change takes effect and is displayed in the table only if the user clicks the Update Row button after editing.

In tables with external editing, a user's changes to a row all take effect at the same time—when the user clicks the Update Row button or the New Row button. For this reason, the values in the row always stay consistent with one another.

Table 9 describes commands for manipulating row-selection tables that are externally editable.

TABLE 9   Commands for Row-Selection Tables with External Editing

Command	Mnemonic	Description
Delete Row	R	Deletes the selected rows.
Move Row Up	U	Moves the selected rows up by one row.
Move Row Down	D	Moves the selected rows down by one row.
Update Row	P	Copies values from the input fields of the editing area into the selected row. The copied values remain displayed in the input fields. If the selection contains more than one row, the Update Row command and the input fields of the editing area are unavailable.
New Row	N	Adds a new row directly above the uppermost selected row or, if there is no selection, adds a new row at the table's end. In either case, the New Row command fills the new row with values from the editing area's input fields and selects the new row. (The values in the editing area remain displayed there.) In addition, the New Row command deselects any previous selection and moves the insertion point to the first editable field of the editing area.
Clear Form	C	Sets each editable component of the editing area to its default value or, if there is no default value, clears the field.

Typically, the commands for manipulating an externally editable row-selection table are divided between two locations—below the table and to the right of it, as shown in Figure 45 on page 69.

When labeling command buttons for an externally editable table, you can use the names Update Row and so on, as in Table 9. Alternatively, you can replace the word "Row" with the name of the object to which the row corresponds.

☕ Use the external editing model in row-selection tables if users must edit each row as a unit.

☕ For externally editable row-selection tables, ensure that table commands work as described in Table 9.

☕ If you use the default names for commands that manipulate externally editable row-selection tables, assign the recommended mnemonics to those commands. (Table 9 lists the default names and the recommended mnemonics.)

☕ For externally editable tables, open an alert box if a user changes values in the table's editing area but then either:

■ Selects a new row without first clicking Update Row or New Row, or
■ Clicks the Clear Form button without first clicking the Update Row button or New Row button.

In the alert box, ask the user to confirm whether the pending changes should be discarded.

Internal Editing Model—The internal editing model enables users to edit a table row by entering values directly in the row's cells. A user's changes to a row take effect one cell at a time, as the user moves keyboard focus from cell to cell. As a result, the values displayed in the row's cells can become temporarily inconsistent with one another while the user edits interdependent cells one at a time.

Figure 46 shows a row-selection table with internal editing.

FIGURE 46   Row-Selection Table with Internal Editing

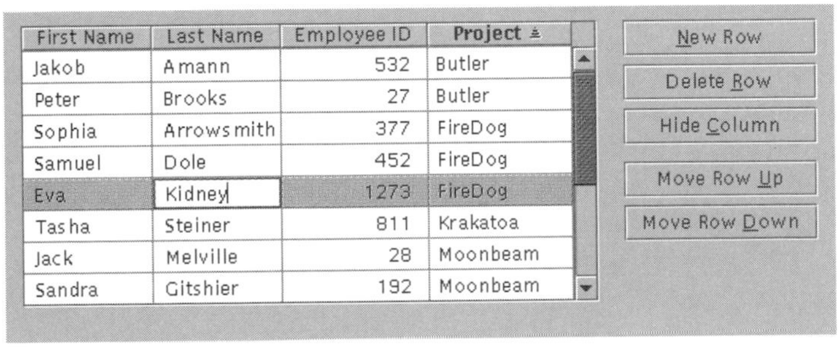

Table 10 describes commands for manipulating row-selection tables that are internally editable.

TABLE 10   Commands for Row-Selection Tables with Internal Editing

Command	Mnemonic	Description
New Row	N	Adds a new row directly above the uppermost row of the selected rows or, if there is no selection, adds a new row at the table's end. In either case, the New Row command selects the new row, deselecting any previous selection, and moves the insertion point to the first editable cell of the new row.
Delete Row	R	Deletes the selected rows.
Hide Column	C	Hides the column that has keyboard focus.
Move Row Up	U	Moves the selected rows up by one row.
Move Row Down	D	Moves the selected rows down by one row.

☕ Provide internally editable row-selection tables if your application must process each row as a unit, but users can edit or copy cells individually.

☕ For internally editable row-selection tables, ensure that table commands work as described in Table 10.

☕ If you use the default names for commands that manipulate internally editable row-selection tables, assign the recommended mnemonics to those commands. (Table 10 lists the default names and the recommended mnemonics.)

Using Cell-Selection Models   You should use a cell-selection model in an application-provided table only if no row-selection model is appropriate. A table that uses a cell selection model is called a cell-selection table.

You can associate commands with a cell-selection table so that users can manipulate its rows and columns. Figure 47 shows a table with such commands, represented as buttons to the right of the table.

FIGURE 47   Cell-Selection Table with Associated Command Buttons

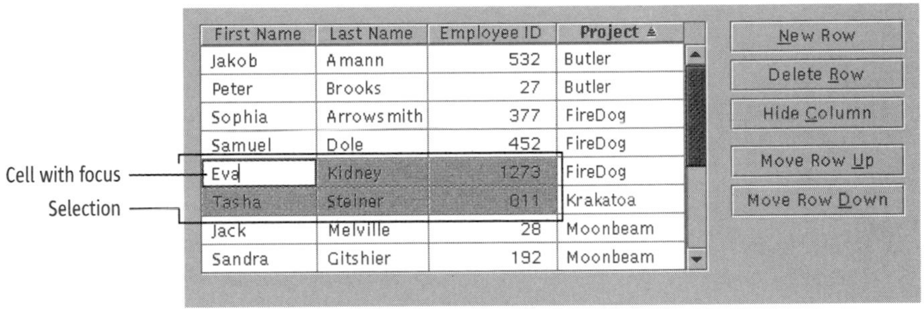

In Figure 47, each command applies to all the rows or columns that contain a selected cell.

Table 11 describes the commands for manipulating cell-selection tables and lists the commands' recommended mnemonics.

TABLE 11   Commands for Cell-Selection Tables

Command	Mnemonic	Description
New Row	N	Adds a new row directly above the uppermost row of the selected cells, or if there is no selection, adds a new row at the table's end. In addition, the New Row command moves the insertion point to the first editable cell of the new row. (Your application should enable users to add a new row at the end of the table—typically, by clicking the Tab key in the final cell of the final row.)
Delete Row	R	Deletes the rows containing the selected cells.
Hide Column	C	Hides the columns containing the selected cells.
Move Row Up	U	Moves the rows containing the selected cells up by one row.
Move Row Down	D	Moves the rows containing the selected cells down by one row.

In Table 11, the commands are not for editing the contents of cells. For information on editing cell contents, see the next section.

When providing commands for manipulating cell-selection tables, include only the commands that users need.

☕ Use a cell-selection model in tables where actions can apply to cells or groups of cells individually.

☕ For cell-selection tables, ensure that table commands work as described in Table 11.

☕ If you use the default names for commands that manipulate cell-selection tables, assign the recommended mnemonics to those commands. (Table 11 lists the default names and the recommended mnemonics.)

☕ If a user deletes a row of a cell-selection table, move the selection to the first cell of a different row. Follow these rules:

- If the deleted row was the table's only row, either:
  - Display the table with a single empty row, in which the first cell is selected, or
  - Display the table with no rows, if the user can add rows.

- If the deleted row was not the table's only row but was the table's bottom row, select the first cell of the row directly above the deleted row.

- If the deleted row was neither the table's only row nor the bottom row, select the first cell of the row directly below the deleted row.

Editing Cell-Selection Tables

You can enable users to edit the contents of cell-selection tables by entering values directly in the cell that has keyboard focus. Figure 48 shows an editable cell-selection table.

FIGURE 48   Editable Cell-Selection Table

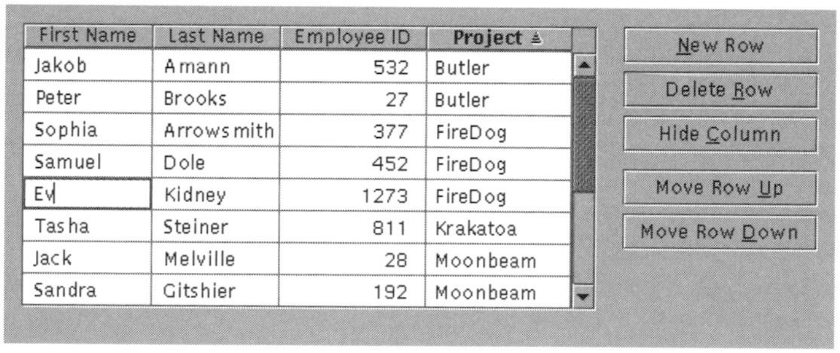

Idioms for Arranging a Table

You can enhance the usability of application-provided tables in your application by consistently using the same idioms. This section describes table idioms for:

- Table appearance
- Table command placement
- Column reordering and resizing
- Row sorting
- Tree tables

Table Appearance

You can increase the visual appeal and readability of your application's tables by using appropriate text formats, background colors, and line settings. This section provides guidelines for defining the appearance of tables.

Figure 49 shows a table that follows the guidelines for appearance. Specific guidelines on table sorting, primary-sort columns, sort indicators, and row striping are provided later in this section.

FIGURE 49   Table Conforming to Guidelines for Appearance

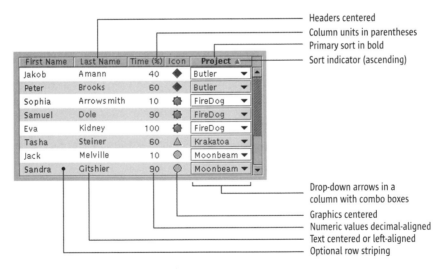

Align the contents of table cells based on their information type. For cells containing numeric values (not character strings with numerals), use decimal alignment. For cells containing long text, use left alignment. For cells containing graphics or short words (like keywords, such as on and off), use center alignment.

☕ Use headline capitalization in column headers of tables. (For a description of headline capitalization, see Chapter 4 of *Java Look and Feel Design Guidelines*, 2d ed.)

☕ Center titles in the column headers of tables, except brief titles of wide text columns that are mostly blank. Center or left-justify brief titles.

☕ In column headers of tables, include the column's unit of measurement as part of the title, and enclose the unit of measurement in parentheses—for example, `CPU Usage(%)`.

☕ In tables, make each column wide enough by default to display the column's title and the contents of typical cells without clipping. In columns where a typical cell's contents are unusually long (for example, a file's full pathname), make the default column width sufficient to display the column's title and the main part of a typical cell's contents—for example, just the file name, clipping the rest of the full pathname. Optionally, if a column header is much longer than the typical contents of the column's cells, you can divide the column header into two or more lines.

☕ Place at least three pixels of blank space between a table cell's contents and the cell's left edge. Likewise, place at least three pixels of blank space between the cell's contents and the cell's right edge.

▤▷ Your application should provide the code for inserting blank space between a table cell's contents and the cell's edges.

Grid Lines and Row Striping   You can often make tables easier to read by using **grid lines** or **row striping**. Grid lines are horizontal or vertical lines that separate a table's rows or columns. Row striping is the technique of using one background color for a table's even-numbered rows and a different background color for its odd-numbered rows.

Not all tables should have grid lines or row striping. For example, most tables with editable fields should not have row striping. Short, noneditable tables listing file names or properties rarely need grid lines or row striping.

The following guidelines help you decide whether to use grid lines, row striping, or neither.

☕ Do not use grid lines and row striping in the same table.

☕ Use horizontal and vertical grid lines in cell-selection tables.

☕ Use horizontal and vertical grid lines in internally editable row-selection tables.

☕ Do not use grid lines in row-selection tables that are noneditable or are externally editable. Instead, use row striping if the table has approximately six columns or more. If the table has fewer columns, use neither grid lines nor row striping.

☕ If a table has grid lines, display them in the color Secondary 2, as described in Chapter 4 of *Java Look and Feel Design Guidelines*, 2d ed.

☕ In tables without grid lines, ensure that there is no space between cells where grid lines would otherwise be.

☕ When striping a table, use light gray (RGB 230-230-230 and Hex #E6E6E6) as the background color of the striped rows (the rows whose background color will not be white).

☕ When striping a table row, stripe all its components. For example, ensure that the row's combo boxes (if any) have the same background color as the rest of the row.

Drop-Down Arrows in Combo Boxes   In tables with cells that contain **combo boxes**, you can sometime enhance table appearance by controlling when **drop-down arrows** are displayed. By default, the drop-down arrow of each combo box is always displayed, as shown in Figure 49 on page 75. Although this default behavior is preferred in most tables, displaying all the drop-down arrows continuously can create clutter in tables with many combo boxes. To avoid clutter, display the drop-down arrow of each combo box only while that box is selected.

For information about where to place table commands, see the next section. For more information on defining the appearance of tables, see Chapter 12 of *Java Look and Feel Design Guidelines*, 2d ed.

☕ If most of a table's cells contain combo boxes, display the drop-down arrow of each combo box only while that box is selected.

Table Command Placement   A table can have associated commands—such as New Row and Move Row Up—that enable users to manipulate the table. Typically, the correct way to represent such commands is as a command button row located either:

- Directly below the table, or
- Directly to the right of the table

Figure 50 shows a table with command buttons directly below it.

FIGURE 50   Table with Command Buttons Below

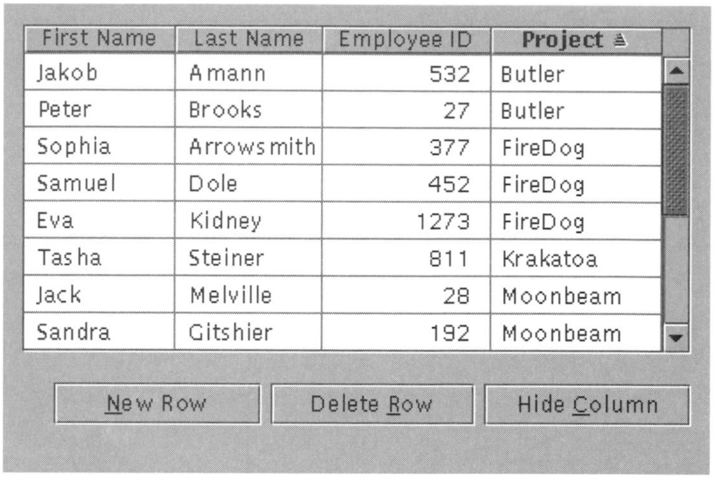

First Name	Last Name	Employee ID	Project ⋚
Jakob	Amann	532	Butler
Peter	Brooks	27	Butler
Sophia	Arrowsmith	377	FireDog
Samuel	Dole	452	FireDog
Eva	Kidney	1273	FireDog
Tasha	Steiner	811	Krakatoa
Jack	Melville	28	Moonbeam
Sandra	Gitshier	192	Moonbeam

[New Row]   [Delete Row]   [Hide Column]

Figure 51 shows a table with command buttons directly on the right.

FIGURE 51   Table with Command Buttons on the Right

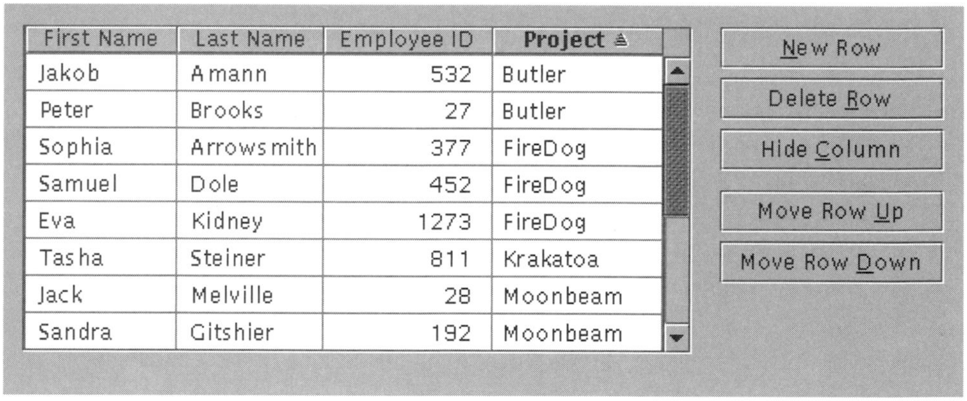

First Name	Last Name	Employee ID	Project ⋚
Jakob	Amann	532	Butler
Peter	Brooks	27	Butler
Sophia	Arrowsmith	377	FireDog
Samuel	Dole	452	FireDog
Eva	Kidney	1273	FireDog
Tasha	Steiner	811	Krakatoa
Jack	Melville	28	Moonbeam
Sandra	Gitshier	192	Moonbeam

[New Row]
[Delete Row]
[Hide Column]
[Move Row Up]
[Move Row Down]

Sometimes, representing table commands as buttons is not practical because
either:

■ The available screen space is too small, or
■ The table is one of several in the same window (the commands' standard
  mnemonics would be ambiguous).

Under such conditions, you can represent a table's commands as menu items
in the window's Edit menu, if there is one. Figure 52 shows table commands
in an Edit menu.

FIGURE 52   Table Commands in a Window's Edit Menu

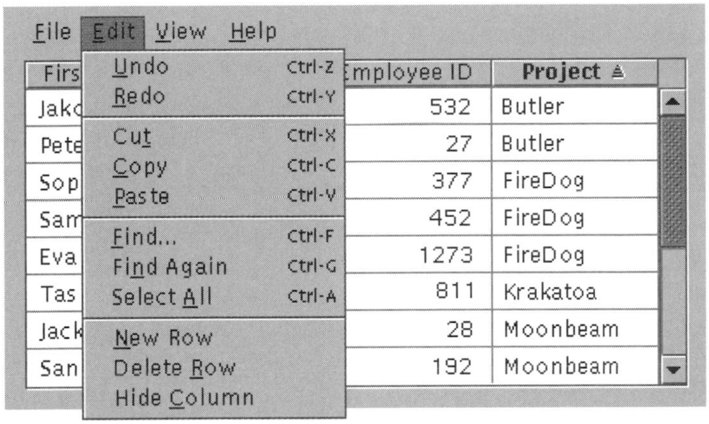

If the Edit menu is too long to include the table commands, you can place them instead in a Table menu in the window as shown in Figure 53.

FIGURE 53   Table Commands in a Window's Table Menu

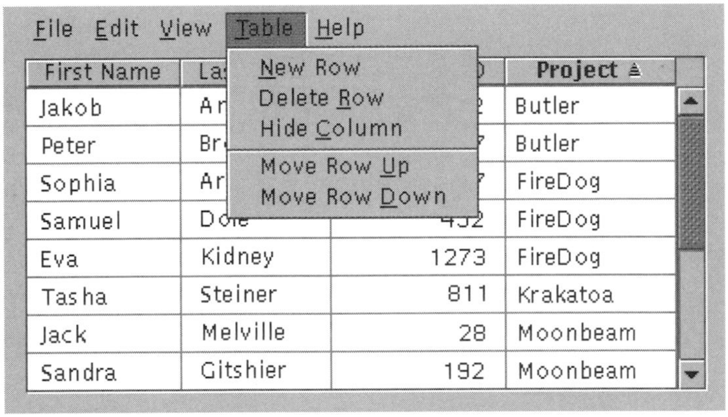

When providing commands for manipulating a table, place them in a command button row directly below the table or directly to the right of it. If you cannot, place the commands in the window's Edit menu or Table menu.

If you place table commands in a menu, also place appropriate table commands in the contextual menus for the table's rows and cells. In addition, you can place table commands in a toolbar.

Column Reordering and Column Resizing   Users sometimes need to reorder a table's columns (by moving them left or right) or resize a table's columns (by changing their width). The following guidelines on column reordering and column resizing supplement those in Chapter 12 of *Java Look and Feel Design Guidelines*, 2d ed.

☕ Enable users to reorder table columns.

☕ If a user reorders a table's columns, use the new column order the next time the user opens that table.

☕ If users can reorder a table's columns, make each column's title unique within the table.

☕ Enable users to change the width of table columns.

☕ If a user changes the widths of a table's columns, use the new widths the next time the user opens that table.

Row Sorting   When viewing a sorted table, users need to know by which columns the table is sorted. These columns are called **sort keys**. To indicate each of a table's sort keys, your application can display a **sort indicator**—a small triangular graphic in the column header. Figure 54 shows sort indicators in the columns of an email application.

FIGURE 54   Sort Indicators in the Columns of a Table

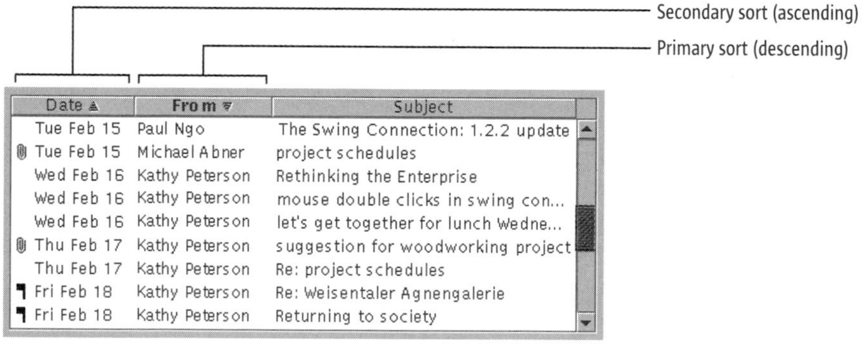

A sort indicator shows that a column is sorted and in which direction — ascending (for example, from A to Z) or descending (for example, from Z to A). An upward-pointing sort indicator indicates an **ascending sort**. A downward-pointing sort indicator indicates a **descending sort**.

A bold column header indicates the table's **primary key**, the main column by which the table is sorted.

You can make each column header a control with the following behavior:

- Clicking a column header makes that column the primary key and sorts the column in the direction that is more useful to users. (Typically, users find an ascending sort more useful.)
- If the column is already the primary key, clicking the column header inverts the current sort, toggling between an ascending sort and a descending sort.

For more information about row sorting, see Chapter 12 of *Java Look and Feel Design Guidelines*, 2d ed.

☕ Enable users to sort tables that typically contain more items than can be displayed at one time.

☕ If a column currently determines a table's sort order, use bold highlighting to display that column's header text. If anything invalidates the sort order, omit the bold highlighting from the column header text. (The column that currently determines a table's sort order is a user's most recently sorted column or, if rows are sorted automatically, the primary-key column.)

☕ In sorted tables, place a sort indicator in each column by which the table is sorted.

☕ In columns with sort indicators, place the sort indicator directly after the column's title.

☕ Omit sort indicators from table columns that, though previously sorted, are no longer sorted.

☕ When sorting a table already sorted by a different column, perform a **stable sort**. In a stable sort, previously sorted rows (if any) retain their positions relative to one another, if they have identical values in the new sort column.

☕ Provide explicit, keyboard-accessible commands for sorting. Ensure that each command operates on the column containing the selection. In tables where users can select a range of cells, make commands for sorting unavailable when the selection includes more than one cell.

☕ When providing sort commands, put them in places consistent with where you put your application's other commands—for example, on buttons, in a toolbar, in a drop-down menu, or in a contextual menu. (For more information, see "Table Command Placement" on page 77.)

Automatic Row Sorting   Your application can provide tables that are automatically sorted each time users edit a row or add one. This feature, called **automatic row sorting**, offers users the convenience of knowing that a table's rows are always sorted.

When providing automatic row sorting, you can enable users to control which table columns are sort keys. In each table, you can enable users to request automatic sorting on a single column (1-column sorting) or on up to *n* columns (*n*-column sorting). Your application sets the value of *n*.

You can enable users to specify the sort columns by, for example, clicking column headers in the table. However, you must also provide a keyboard-accessible alternative. For *n*-column sorting, you can enable users to specify sort columns by opening a dialog box from a menu item or a button.

Tables with automatic row sorting should conform to all guidelines for row sorting and to the following guidelines for automatic row sorting.

☕ Provide automatic row sorting in tables unless doing so would slow your application's response—as when tables are too large to sort quickly.

☕ Sort a row automatically only if keyboard focus is not in that row.

☕ In tables with automatic row sorting, enable users to choose which columns are used as sort keys.

Tree Table Idiom   A **tree table** is a table in which the leftmost column is a tree of objects, one object to a row, and the other columns consist of rows that describe the corresponding object in the tree. Figure 55 shows a tree table. You can use a tree table to display two or more properties of each object in a tree.

FIGURE 55   Tree Table

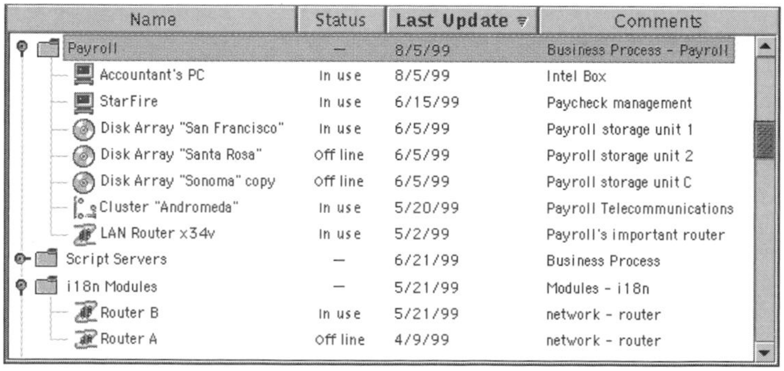

In tree tables, each object in the tree is either a **leaf node** (such as a file) or a **container** (such as a folder). A container can contain leaf nodes and other containers. Users can expand or collapse rows for containers to show or hide rows for the container's contents.

Figure 56 shows containers and leaf nodes in a tree table.

FIGURE 56   Containers and Leaf Nodes in a Tree Table

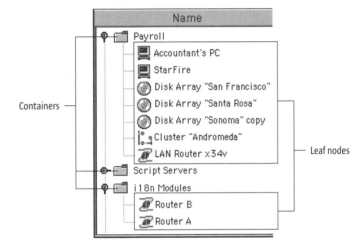

Tree tables have many features in common with other kinds of tables. For example, you can enable users of tree tables to:

- Select a group of rows
- Resize columns
- Edit the contents of cells individually
- Sort rows

By default, tree tables enable users to select only a single row. Selecting a row that corresponds to a container does not select rows for the container's contents. Moving or copying a container's row within a tree table also moves or copies the rows for the container's contents. Likewise, deleting a container's row from a tree table also deletes the rows for the container's contents.

You can enable users to sort the rows of a tree table. The default sort is hierarchical. It sorts leaf nodes and containers as a single set, with each container's contents sorted under that container.

In some applications, users might need to sort all rows of a tree table as a single set, ignoring whether rows are for containers or leaf nodes. You can provide this capability by enabling users to convert a tree table into a non-hierarchical table. If you provide this capability, also provide a separate command for performing the conversion.

The following guidelines apply to tree tables.

☕ Use a row selection model, typically with internal editing. (For more information, see "Using Row-Selection Models" on page 67 and "Editing Row-Selection Tables" on page 69.)

☕ Enable users to sort the table by clicking its column headers. In addition, provide a keyboard-accessible command for sorting the table.

☕ When sorting tree tables, sort hierarchically, based on each object's level in the tree.

☕ Enable users to change the width of table columns.

☕ If a user changes the width of a table column, use the new width the next time the user opens that table.

☕ Do not place vertical grid lines between the columns of a tree table. (You can, however, place horizontal grid lines between a tree table's rows.)

▤▻ For information on tree tables, including example code, see:
`http://java.sun.com/products/jfc/tsc/articles/`
`treetable1/index.html`

Idioms for Text Fields and Lists   You can use the following idioms to help users work with text fields and lists:

- Browse
- Key-Search
- Add-and-Remove

Browse Idiom   The Browse idiom enables users to specify an object—typically, a file, directory, or web page. This idiom consists of a label, an editable text field, and a command button, whose text begins with the word "Browse," as shown in Figure 57.

FIGURE 57   Browse Idiom

In the Browse idiom, users can enter data into the text field by either:

- Typing in the text field, or
- Clicking the command button to choose text from a list in a dialog box

Clicking the command button opens a dialog box that enables users to navigate through a hierarchy of locations and then choose a file, directory, web page, or other object. Typically, choosing an object causes the text field to display the full path to that object.

☞ Use the Browse idiom to enable users to specify a file, directory, web address, or other item in a very large set.

☞ When using the Browse idiom for choosing a file, directory, or web address, label the idiom's command button "Browse," and use "B" as its mnemonic unless that letter is a mnemonic for different button or command.

☞ In a window with more than one copy of the Browse idiom, assign different button text and a different mnemonic to each copy's command button. For example, you could make one button's text Browse For Template and another button's text Browse For Message Folder. Even if you cannot make each button's text different from the others, use a different mnemonic for each button.

Key-Search Idiom   You can help users find list items faster in your application by using the **Key-Search idiom** in lists, combo boxes, and trees. Figure 58 shows an example use of the Key-Search idiom.

The Key-Search idiom enables users to find a list item by typing its first letter (called the "search key" or "key"). The Key-Search idiom is case insensitive, and it works on any list of text items, even an unsorted list.

To start a key search, a user types any printable character while keyboard focus is in a list. In response, the application deselects the currently selected list item and then scrolls down to the next list item that begins with that character, highlighting that item. For example, if the user types the letter **v**, the key search highlights the next item that begins with **V** or **v**, as shown on the left in Figure 58.

FIGURE 58   Two Successive Key Searches on the Letter "v"

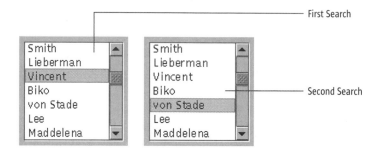

To find each subsequent list item that begins with **v** or **v**, the user types the letter **v** again. The right side of Figure 58 shows the result of typing **v** after the first search, shown on the left. Successive searches on the same key cause the application to loop through the list until the user stops searching.

If a search key does not match the first character of any list item, the application should alert the user—for example, by causing the user's system to beep—but should leave the current highlighting and selection unchanged.

☕ Use the Key-Search idiom in any list that might become long enough to require vertical scrolling.

🖘 As of version 1.4 of the Java 2 SDK, the key-search feature is part of the standard behavior for components that extend the `JList`, `JComboBox`, or `JTree` class.

Add-and-Remove Idiom   To enable users to choose a subset from a large list of objects, you can provide the **Add-and-Remove idiom**. This idiom consists of two lists separated by a command-button row, as shown in Figure 59.

FIGURE 59   Add-and-Remove Idiom

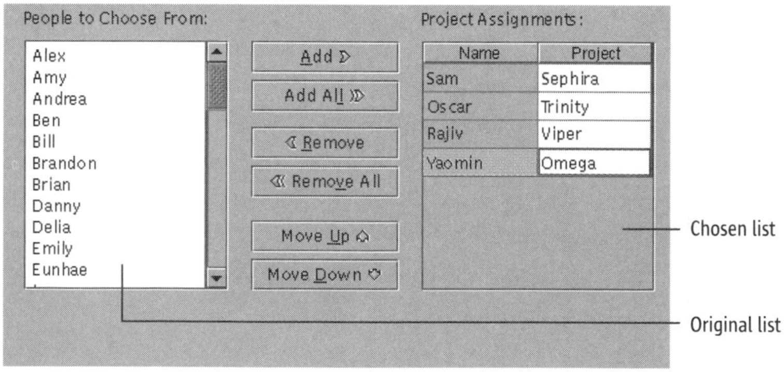

The list on the left, called the **original list**, contains a set of objects that users can add to the list on the right—the **chosen list**. The command buttons enable users to control which items appear in the chosen list. In Figure 59:

- The original list is labeled "People to Choose From."
- The chosen list is labeled "Project Assignments."

Optionally, the chosen list can be a table, as in Figure 59. The table's leftmost column, called the **main column**, displays items that come from the original list. In Figure 59, the Name column is the main column.

The chosen list can have one or more **supplementary columns** to provide more information about each item in the main column. In Figure 59, the Project column is the only supplementary column.

Supplementary columns can be noneditable or editable:

- Noneditable supplementary columns display information about chosen-list items.
- Editable supplementary columns enable users to set parameters for this table's use of each chosen-list item.

☕ Provide the Add-and-Remove idiom if users need to choose a few objects from a long list.

☕ In the Add-and-Remove idiom, make the chosen list a table only if the supplementary columns hold either:

- Noneditable data, or
- User-input fields for parameters regarding this table's use of each chosen-list item

☕ In the Add-and-Remove idiom, if the chosen list is a table, use a row-selection model. If the table is editable, use internal editing. (For more information, see "Using Row-Selection Models" on page 67 and "Editing Row-Selection Tables" on page 69.)

Commands in the Add-and-Remove Idiom   Table 12 describes the command buttons that
you can include in the Add-and-Remove idiom.

TABLE 12   Command Buttons for the Add-and-Remove Idiom

Button Text	Mnemonic	Description
A̲dd	A	Adds items to the chosen list. The Add command copies all selected items from the original list and adds them to the chosen list—at the end or, if the chosen list is sorted, in their correct positions. If the items must be unique in the chosen list, the Add command then deletes from the original list all copied items. Finally, the Add command selects the copied items in the chosen list and deselects any previously selected items in the original list. The Add command is available only while one or more items are selected in the original list. Another way to activate the Add command is to double-click an item in the original list, thereby selecting it and immediately adding it to the chosen list.
Add A̲ll	L	(Optional) Moves or copies all items from the original list to the chosen list and then selects them in the chosen list. The Add All command is available only while the original list is not empty. You should provide the Add All command only if your users need it.
R̲emove	R	Removes items from the chosen list. The Remove command removes the selected items from the chosen list, adds them to the original list (at the end or, preferably, at their previous positions), and, finally, selects the items in the original list, deselecting the chosen list. Removing an item from the chosen list has no effect on the original list if that item is already in the original list. The Remove command is available only while one or more items are selected in the chosen list.
Remo̲ve All	V	(Optional) Moves all items from the chosen list to the original list. The Remove All command is available only while the chosen list is not empty.
Move U̲p	U	(Optional) Moves the selected items one row up in the chosen list. If a user applies the Move Up command to a selection containing nonadjacent items, the command works as if the user performed it on each of the items separately. As a result, the items retain their positions relative to one another.
Move D̲own	D	(Optional) Moves the selected items one row down in the chosen list.

☕ In the Add-and-Remove idiom, ensure that the command buttons
behave as described in Table 12.

☕ In the Add-and-Remove idiom, provide the Add All command only if you
also provide the Remove All command. (You can provide the Remove All
command without also providing the Add All command.)

☕ Assign the mnemonics in Table 12 to the command buttons of the Add-and-Remove idiom.

☕ When adding list items in the Add-and-Remove idiom, display at least the first newly added item, by scrolling the list if necessary.

Button Graphics in the Add-and-Remove Idiom   In the Add-and-Remove idiom, you can label command buttons with a graphic and text, or with just a graphic. The correct choice depends on the type of users and the amount of available space.

☕ In the Add-and-Remove idiom, label the command buttons with a graphic and text—especially if your application's users are inexperienced with computers. Label the command buttons with just a graphic only if there is no space for text and your application's users are experienced.

☕ In the Add-and-Remove idiom, provide tool tips for the command buttons if the buttons are labeled with just a graphic.

Layout of the Add-and-Remove Idiom   Typically, the command buttons of the Add-and-Remove idiom are between the original list and the chosen list. The buttons are spaced as shown in Figure 60. Measurements in the figure are in pixels.

FIGURE 60   Preferred Layout of the Add-and-Remove Idiom

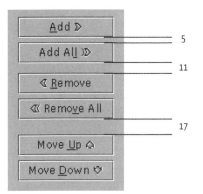

In windows without enough vertical space for the typical layout, you can lay out the Add-and-Remove Idiom as shown in Figure 61. In the figure, the Move Up and Move Down buttons are to the right of the chosen list and apply only to that list.

FIGURE 61   Layout of the Add-and-Remove Idiom with Limited Vertical Space

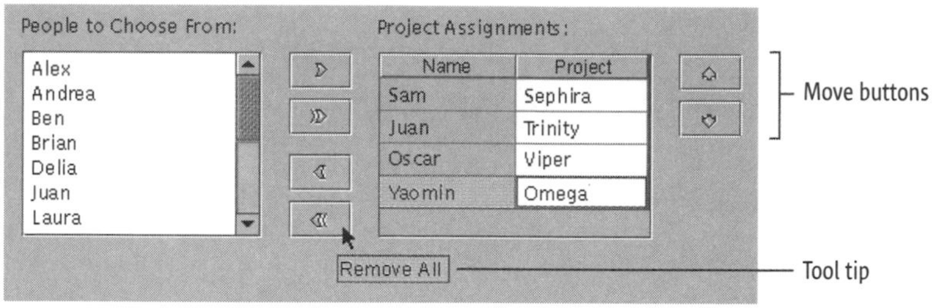

In the Add-and-Remove idiom, arrange and order the command buttons as shown in Figure 60 on page 89. In windows without enough vertical space, use the layout shown in Figure 61.

In the Add-and-Remove idiom, make the vertical space for the original list at least as long as the column of command buttons, as shown in Figure 61. Provide the same amount of vertical space for the chosen list as for the original list.

Container-and-Contents Idiom

Users sometimes need to view a hierarchy of containers—for example, a set of file folders—while also viewing the contents of a selected container—for example, the list of documents in a selected folder. You can provide this capability by using the **Container-and-Contents idiom**, which consists of a **split pane** displaying a different view in each of its two panes:

- The left pane contains a **tree component** displaying a hierarchy of containers, one of which is selected. The left pane's selected container can contain leaf nodes as well as subcontainers.
- The right pane contains a table or a set of icons representing the contents of the left pane's selected container. (A set of icons in a pane is known as an **icon pane**.)

For a description of split panes, see Chapter 7 of *Java Look and Feel Design Guidelines*, 2d ed.

Figure 62 shows the Container-and-Contents idiom used in the upper two panes of an email application.

FIGURE 62   Container-and-Contents Idiom in an Email Application

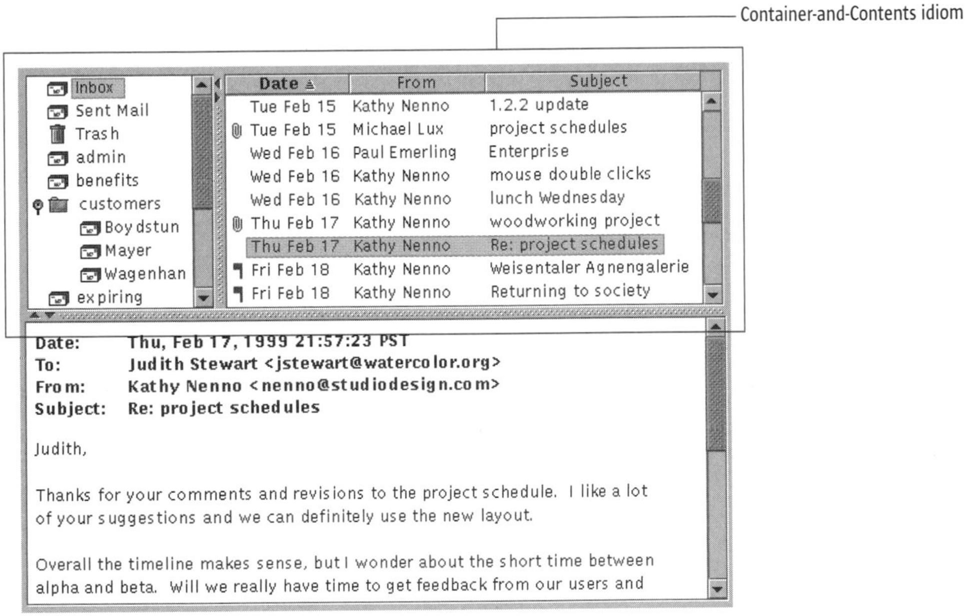

In the Container-and-Contents idiom, the left and right panes work together. Changing the selection in the left pane (the tree) changes which object's contents are displayed in the right pane (the table).

In the right pane, if a user opens a subcontainer:

- That subcontainer becomes highlighted in the left and right panes.
- Highlighting is removed from the left pane's previously highlighted item.

In Figure 62, the right pane displays the contents of only one container—labeled Inbox in the left pane—so this behavior does not apply to the figure.

The container-and-contents uses a single-selection model—that is, the selection can contain only one object at the time, although that object can be a container.

The following guidelines apply to the Container-and-Contents idiom.

☕ Ensure that clicking a container in the left pane causes the right pane to display that container's contents.

☕ Ensure that double-clicking a collapsed container in the left pane expands that container and makes its subnodes visible in the right pane. Likewise, ensure that double-clicking an expanded container in the left pane collapses that container and causes its subnodes to be become visible in the right pane.

6: RESPONSIVENESS

Responsiveness, as defined by Jeff Johnson in his book *GUI Bloopers: Don'ts and Do's for Software Developers and Web Designers*, is "the software's ability to keep up with users and not make them wait." Responsiveness is often cited as the strongest factor in users' satisfaction with software applications and has been linked to users' productivity, as well.

Poor responsiveness can render an otherwise well-designed application unusable. Maximizing the responsiveness of your application is among the best ways that you can improve its usability and help ensure its success.

This chapter provides guidelines for designing responsiveness into your application. To help you understand the guidelines, the chapter also:

- Lists characteristics of responsive applications and problems of unresponsive ones
- Explains how responsiveness relates to performance and response delay
- Describes ways to measure response delays
- Describes ways to improve responsiveness and provide operational feedback to users

This chapter draws heavily from the work of usability expert Jeff Johnson. To learn more about how to design for responsiveness, read his book *GUI Bloopers*. This chapter also draws from the work of performance experts Steve Wilson and Jeff Kesselman. For a discussion of responsiveness as it relates to performance, read their book *Java Platform Performance: Strategies and Tactics*. These books are described in "Related Books" on page xiv.

Characteristics of Responsive Applications

Although highly responsive applications can differ widely from one another, they share the following characteristics:

- They keep up with users, even when they cannot fulfill users' requests immediately.
- They handle queued requests as users would expect—discarding requests that are no longer relevant and reordering requests according to users' probable priorities.

- They let users do other work while long operations proceed to completion—especially operations not requested by users, such as reclaiming unused memory or other "housekeeping" operations.
- They provide enough feedback for users to understand what they are doing, and they organize feedback according to users' abilities to comprehend and react to it.
- They let users know when processing is in progress.
- They let users know or estimate how long lengthy operations will take.
- They let users set the pace of work, when possible, and they let users stop requested tasks that have begun but not finished.

Highly responsive applications put users in control by quickly acknowledging each user request, by providing continuous feedback about progress toward fulfilling each request, and by letting users complete tasks without unacceptable delays.

Problems of Unresponsive Applications   Even applications
with attractive, intuitive user interfaces can lack responsiveness. Typically, unresponsive applications have at least one the following problems:

- They provide late feedback—or no feedback—for users' requests, leaving users puzzled about what the application has done or is doing.
- When performing extended operations, they prevent users from doing other work or canceling the extended operation.
- They fail to display estimates of how long extended operations will last, forcing users to wait for unpredictable periods.
- They ignore users' requests while doing unrequested "housekeeping," forcing users to wait at unpredictable times—often without feedback.

Each of these problems can frustrate users and lower their productivity.

Responsiveness as Part of Performance   In *Java Platform*
Performance, coauthors Steve Wilson and Jeff Kesselman describe performance as a general term for several related measurements, among them:

- Computational performance
- Scalability
- Perceived performance, which this chapter calls "responsiveness"

Computational Performance   **Computational performance**—what software engineers usually mean by "performance"—focuses on fast algorithms, efficient data structures, and economical use of processor time.

Responsiveness and computational performance are not always related. Improving the computational performance of an application improves its responsiveness only if users prefer the change or if the change increases users' speed or accuracy.

It is sometimes possible to improve an application's responsiveness without speeding up the application's code. For tips on how to make such improvements, see "Responding to User Requests" on page 98.

Scalability   The term **scalability** has two meanings:

- In the context of computational performance, scalability is an application's ability to perform under heavy loads—for example, large numbers of concurrent users.
- In the context of user interfaces, scalability is the ability of a user interface to remain responsive as a user:
  - Does increasingly complex work
  - Tries to gain access to increasing numbers of interface objects—for example, file folders or device descriptions

Without a scalable user interface and scalability in performance, an application can quickly fall from being highly responsive to being extremely unresponsive.

Perceived Performance, or Responsiveness   **Perceived performance**, or **responsiveness**, is based on how fast an application seems to its users—how well it responds to them, not necessarily how fast it fulfills their requests.

Determining Acceptable Response Delays   The term
response delay refers to how long an application takes to acknowledge or fulfill a particular user request. Providing responsiveness in an application depends on achieving response delays that are acceptable to users. The longer an application's response delays are, the more time that its users lose when they make errors—especially if those errors are hard to correct. Anxiety about making time-consuming errors can frustrate users, causing them to work more slowly yet make more errors because they lose their concentration.

Inappropriately short response delays can cause problems, too. For example, one such problem occurs if an application displays and erases a message faster than users can read it. If an application displays and erases successive sets of information faster than users can read them or respond to them, users nonetheless try to keep up. As a result, they make more errors, because the application, though fast, does not keep pace with its users.

Some user interface events require shorter response delays than others. For example, an application's response to a user's mouse click or key press needs to be much faster than its response to a request to save a file. Table 13 shows the maximum acceptable response delay for typical interface events.

TABLE 13   Maximum Acceptable Response Delays for Typical Events

User Interface Events	Maximum Acceptable Response Delay
Mouse click; pointer movement; window movement or resizing; key press; button press; drawing gesture; other user-input event involving hand-eye coordination	0.1 second (100 milliseconds)
Displaying progress indicators; completing ordinary user commands (for example, closing a dialog box); completing background tasks (for example, reformatting a table)	1.0 second
Displaying a graph or anything else that a typical user would expect to take time (for example, displaying a new list of all a company's financial transactions for an accounting period)	10.0 seconds
Accepting and processing all user input to any task	10.0 seconds

In your application, make each response delay as short as possible, unless users need time to see the displayed information before it is erased. ("Tools for Measuring Response Delays" on page 98 describes techniques for measuring response delays in your application.)

The acceptable response delay for each event is based on a typical user's sense that the event is a logical point at which to stop or pause. The greater that sense is, the more willingly the user will wait for a response.

Verify that your application responds to users' requests within the limits listed in Table 13. If the application cannot respond within those limits, it probably has one or more general problems—ones caused by a particular algorithm or module. To find such problems, analyze the entire application in detail.

For example, one problem might be that your application requires a more powerful computer system than the one on which it was tested. If so, work with your marketing representative to determine the true minimum system requirements for your application.

☕ Verify that your application provides feedback within 100 milliseconds (0.1 second) after each key press, movement of the mouse, or other physical input from the user.

☕ Verify that your application provides feedback within 100 milliseconds (0.1 second) after each change in the state of controls that react to input from the user—for example, displaying menus or indicating drop targets.

☕ Verify that your application takes no longer than 1 second to display each progress indicator, complete each ordinary user command, or complete each background task.

☕ Verify that your application takes no longer than 10 seconds to accept and process all user input to any task—including user input to each step of a multistep task, such as a wizard.

Measuring Response Delays

An application's user interface must respond in real time. To measure objectively how quickly your application responds, you need to measure its response delays. This section describes techniques for quantitatively measuring your application's response delays.

Setting Benchmarks for Response Delays

Measurements of response delays are useful only in relation to benchmarks. A **benchmark** is a goal that you devise to determine whether your application provides acceptable response delays for a specific task. Without benchmarks, you cannot know for sure whether your application is responsive enough.

Establish benchmarks early in your project by reaching a consensus with representative users and your development team—including management, marketing, and engineers. Your goals for acceptable response delays should be reachable on the minimum computer system that your application supports.

Establish qualitative goals only if your team cannot agree on quantitative goals. For example, a qualitative goal might be to scroll smoothly.

Tools for Measuring Response Delays   One tool for objectively measuring response delays is a stopwatch. As Wilson and Kesselman explain in *Java Platform Performance*, testing with a stopwatch has advantages and disadvantages. It is easy to use but is hard to use accurately. In addition, testing with a stopwatch is hard to automate.

A stopwatch is inadequate for measuring milliseconds—which you need to measure when complying with the guidelines in the section "Perceived Performance, or Responsiveness" on page 95. Typically, measuring response delays to the millisecond requires that engineers include tests in the source code of their applications. For text and code examples describing this technique, see the book *Java Platform Performance*.

Responding to User Requests   If an application takes too long to respond, users become frustrated. Here are some techniques that you and your development team can use to improve the responsiveness of your application.

- **Display feedback as soon as possible.**
  - If you cannot display all the information that a user has requested, display the most important information first.
  - Save time by displaying approximate results while calculating finished results.
  - If users are likely to repeat a time-consuming command in rapid succession, save time by faking the command's effects instead of repeatedly processing the command. For example, if a user adds several rows to a table stored in a database, you might display each new row immediately but delay actually creating each new row in the database until the user finished adding all the rows.

- **Work ahead.** Prepare to perform the command that is most likely to follow the current command. That is, use idle time to anticipate users' probable next requests. For example, as the user of an email application reads the currently displayed new message, the application might prepare to display the next new message.

- **Use background processing.** Perform less important tasks—such as housekeeping—in the background, enabling users to continue working.

- **Delay work that is not urgent.** Perform it later, when more time is available.

- **Discard unnecessary operations.** Discard operations that a user has requested but that are not necessary. For example, to move back several pages in a web browser, a user might click the browser's Back button several times in rapid succession. To display the final requested page more quickly, the browser might not display the pages visited between the current page and that final page.

- **Use dynamic time management.** At run time, change how your application prioritizes user input and other processing, based on the application's current state. For example, if a user is typing text in one word-processing document while printing another, the word-processing application might delay the printing task if the user shifts to an editing task (such as cutting and pasting text) that requires greater resources. (For more information on dynamic time management, see the book *GUI Bloopers*.)

Some user requests—for example, scrolling—require a high degree of responsiveness. If your application includes scrolling controls, such as scrollbars or panning controls, make sure that the application's scrolling lets users easily detect in which direction scrolled information is moving. Scrolling should be smooth and should keep pace with the user's ability to scan the information. In addition, the user should be able to stop without overshooting the intended target.

☕ In your application, display an estimate of how long each lengthy operation will take.

☕ If a command might take longer than five seconds to complete its work on an object, enable users to interact with any parts of the object and parts of the application that are not directly affected by the command.

☕ If a command provides lengthy output, show partial results as they become available. Scroll the results (if necessary) until the user moves input focus to a component (such as a scrollbar or text area) involved in the scrolling.

Providing Operational Feedback

Responsive applications provide feedback—including visual feedback—about the state of operations in progress. This section describes:

- How to decide whether to provide feedback for an operation
- Which types of visual feedback you can provide
- How to choose the correct type of visual feedback

For general information on how to provide operational feedback in your application, see Chapter 6 of *Java Look and Feel Design Guidelines*, 2d ed. Also see that chapter for general information about pointer feedback.

Deciding Whether to Provide Feedback   Whether your application should provide feedback on an operation depends on how long that operation usually takes.

To decide whether to provide feedback on an operation, test how long the operation usually takes on the minimum system configuration that your application supports. Repeat the test at least ten times, with different data sets or network loads. Provide feedback if the operation takes longer than one second in at least 10% of the tests.

Types of Visual Feedback   You can use two types of visual feedback for operations in your application—**pointer feedback** and **progress animations**:

- Pointer feedback changes the shape of the pointer. (The pointer tracks movements of the user's mouse or other pointing device.) For example, a wait pointer indicates that an operation is in progress and that the user cannot do other tasks.
- Progress animations show either:
    - How much of an operation is complete, or
    - Only that an operation is ongoing (such animations are also known as **status animations**)

Progress Animations   To provide feedback with a progress animation, an application can display a **progress bar** or a **progress checklist**.

- A progress bar shows how much of the operation is complete (a **measured-progress bar**) or only that the operation is ongoing (an **indeterminate-progress bar**). "Measured- and Indeterminate-Progress Bars" on page 102 describes each type of progress bar in detail.
- A progress checklist shows the sequence of stages in an operation but does not display time estimates for those stages.

NOTE – Except where noted, the term "progress bars" refers to measured-progress bars.

Figure 63 shows a progress bar in a wizard page.

FIGURE 63   Progress Bar (in a Wizard Page)

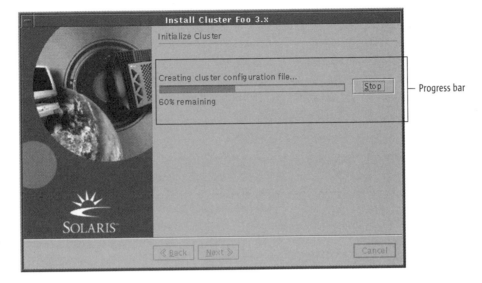

Figure 64 shows a progress checklist, also in a wizard page.

FIGURE 64   Progress Checklist (in a Wizard Page)

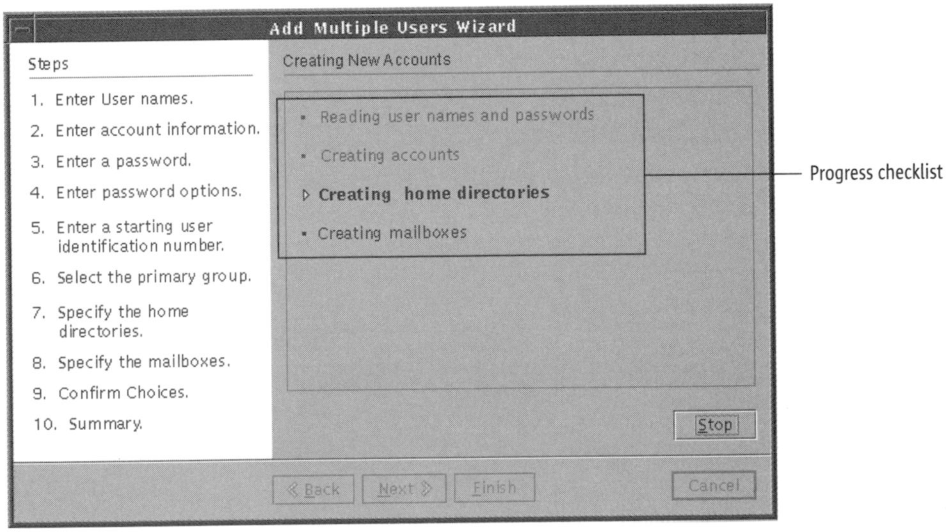

Figure 65 shows an indeterminate-progress bar. (For information about wizards, see Chapter 7. For information about feedback in wizards, see "Providing Operational Feedback in Wizards" on page 141.)

FIGURE 65   Indeterminate-Progress Bar

When providing feedback with a progress checklist, you can include a measured-progress bar directly below the checklist. The bar measures the progress of the current step in the progress checklist.

When displaying a progress animation, your application should open it as quickly as possible and close it automatically as soon as the associated operation is complete.

☕ When providing a progress animation, use a measured-progress bar if your application can estimate either:

- How long the operation will take, or
- What proportion of the operation is complete

If your application can make neither estimate, use an indeterminate-progress bar for operations with only one step. For operations with two or more steps, use a progress checklist that dynamically displays a check mark for each completed step.

☕ Ensure that a measured-progress bar measures an operation's total time or total work, not just that of a single step. An exception is a progress bar that measures the total time or work of the current step in a progress checklist.

Measured- and Indeterminate-Progress Bars   You can use two main types of progress bars in your application—measured-progress bars and indeterminate-progress bars. Measured-progress bars can be classified into the following types:

- Time-remaining bars
- Proportion-completed bars
- Typical-time bars

There is only one type of indeterminate-progress bar.

Table 14 describes each type of progress bar.

TABLE 14   Types of Measured- and Indeterminate-Progress Bars

Type of Progress Bar	Description
Time-remaining	An animation consisting of: • A bar whose changing length indicates how much time remains in an operation • Text stating how much time remains before the operation will be complete Time-remaining bars are the most useful type of progress bar. Figure 63 on page 101 shows a time-remaining bar.
Proportion-completed	A bar whose changing length represents the completed proportion — typically a percentage — of an operation's total units of work. Proportion-completed bars are less useful than time-remaining bars but more useful than typical-time bars.
Typical-time	A bar whose changing length indicates how much time remains if an operation takes as long as it typically does. Typical-time bars are the least precise type of measured-progress bar, but they are more useful than indeterminate-progress bars.
Indeterminate-progress	An animated bar indicating only that an operation is ongoing. Indeterminate-progress bars are the least precise type of progress bar. Figure 65 on page 102 shows an indeterminate-progress bar.

The correct type of bar to use depends on how precisely your application can estimate the duration of the operation in progress.

Progress Bars for More Predictable Durations   If your application can estimate how long a particular instance of an operation will take, you can provide feedback with one the following types of progress bar:

- A time-remaining bar
- A proportion-completed bar

You can use a time-remaining bar if your application will display an initial estimate of an operation's remaining time and then periodically display updated estimates. Each updated estimate should be based on changes that have occurred and that will cause the operation to finish more quickly or more slowly. If the operation will finish more slowly, your application can display an updated estimate that is greater than the estimate previously displayed.

You can use a proportion-completed bar if your application will estimate an operation's duration by counting the units of work completed so far, without regard for changes that might affect how quickly the remaining units will be completed. If the operation will process a known number of objects or a set of objects whose total size is known, equate the length of the bar to the total number of units of work that the operation will perform. At least every four seconds, update the bar to show how much of the operation is complete.

Progress Bars for Less Predictable Durations   For some operations, you cannot estimate the time remaining or the proportion of work completed. However, if you can estimate the typical time for that operation, you can provide feedback with a typical-time bar.

If your application overestimates the completed amount of work, the length of the bar can indicate "almost complete" until the operation is complete. If your application underestimates how much work is complete, the application can fill the remaining portion of the bar when the operation is complete.

You can use an indeterminate-progress bar to provide feedback on an operation whose duration you cannot estimate at all.

For general information about progress bars, see Chapter 6 of *Java Look and Feel Design Guidelines*, 2d ed.

☕ Use the most precise type of progress bar for the operation that you are timing. For a list and description of types, see Table 14.

Providing the Correct Type of Visual Feedback   To determine which type of visual feedback to provide for a particular operation, consider these factors:

- Whether your application can provide an estimate of the operation's progress
- Whether the operation blocks the user from issuing further commands in your application
- Whether your application has a dedicated space—such as an area at the bottom of a window—for indicating the status of operations

Table 15 shows which type of feedback your application should provide for operations that usually take at least one second to finish. In Table 15:

- **Internal progress animations** are progress animations displayed in an application's dedicated status area.
- **External progress animations** are progress animations displayed somewhere other than in a dedicated status area—typically, in an alert box.

TABLE 15   Visual Feedback Types for Operations That Take at Least One Second

Current operation usually takes less than five seconds?	User blocked from issuing further commands?	Application has dedicated area to show status?	Appropriate feedback for current operation is...
✓	✓	✓	Internal progress animation and pointer feedback
✓	✓	—	Pointer feedback
✓	—	✓	Internal progress animation
✓	—	—	Best provided by adding a status area.
—	✓	✓	Internal progress animation and pointer feedback
—	✓	—	External progress animation and pointer feedback
—	—	✓	Internal progress animation
—	—	—	External progress animation

☕ When providing feedback for operations that take at least one second, follow the rules in Table 15.

☕ Use a wait pointer in your user interface whenever users are blocked from interaction with your application for one second or longer. Display the wait pointer in less than one second.

Letting Users Stop Commands in Progress   Users sometimes need to stop a command—for example, because it is taking too long. Your application should let users stop commands in progress—even if stopping a command cannot undo, or "roll back," all the command's effects.

To let users stop a command, place a Stop button near the progress animation for that command. (For more information, see "Progress Animations" on page 100.) Alternatively, you can place the Stop button near the user-interface control with which the user issued the command that needs to be stopped. Place the Stop button in this alternative location only if either:

- There is no progress animation for command, or
- The progress animation is in a window's status area or in another location that lacks space for a Stop button.

If a user clicks the Stop button, the effect should depend on whether terminating a command can have unwanted consequences—also known as **side effects**—such as an incomplete rollback of changes.

Table 16 describes how to decide the correct behavior for the Stop button.

TABLE 16   Correct Behavior for a Stop Button That Stops a Command

Will terminating the command have unwanted consequences?	Clicking the Stop button should...
No	Immediately terminate the command.
Yes	Open an alert box that warns of potential side effects. The alert box should have only two buttons: • A button for continuing the command's processing, canceling the request to terminate it • A button for immediately terminating the command's processing, despite potential side effects

If clicking the Stop button opens an alert box, the button labels of the alert box should be specific and precise. Ambiguous button labels can cause users to terminate or continue a command unintentionally.

Figure 66 shows an alert box for terminating a command.

FIGURE 66   Alert Box for Terminating a Command

If a command will likely take ten seconds or longer to finish, provide a Stop button that lets users terminate the command's processing—even if your application cannot undo the command's effects.

If stopping a partially completed command will not undo all the command's effects, display an alert box to warn users. Ensure that the alert box includes two buttons that enable users to choose between continuing the partially completed command or terminating the command regardless of the side effects. Label each button of the alert box as specifically as possible, for example: `Continue Deleting Files` and `Stop Deleting Files`.

PART II: SPECIAL TOPICS

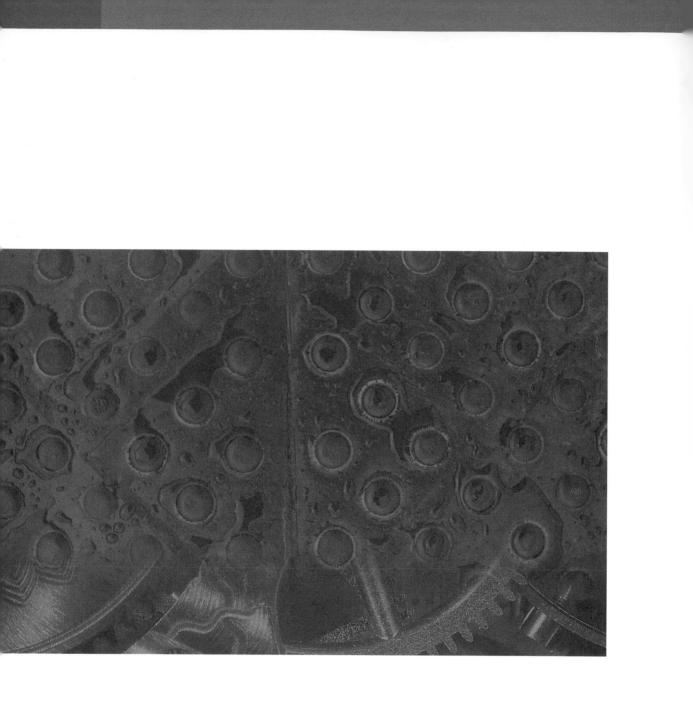

7: WIZARDS

Even in well-designed software, complex or unfamiliar tasks can be difficult. You can make performing difficult tasks easier and quicker for users by providing a kind of user interface known as a wizard.

A **wizard** is a window that leads a user through a task one step at a time— requesting a series of responses from the user and then performing the task based on those responses. Except for a user's responses, a wizard provides all the information needed to perform the task. Typically, wizards are intended to simplify a task so that inexperienced users can perform it easily, or to expedite a complex task by grouping its steps in a single place. Often, wizards both simplify a task and expedite it.

This chapter introduces wizards and then describes:

- How to decide whether users need a wizard
- How to design the layout and behavior of wizards

Wizards have much in common with other types of windows. For general information on windows, see Chapter 2. For general information on layout, visual alignment, and text in the user interface, see Chapter 4 of *Java Look and Feel Design Guidelines*, 2d ed.

Fundamentals of Wizards

A wizard consists of a series of pages in a window. Each page represents a step, or a portion of a step, in a user's task. Figure 67 shows a typical wizard page.

FIGURE 67   Anatomy of a Wizard Page

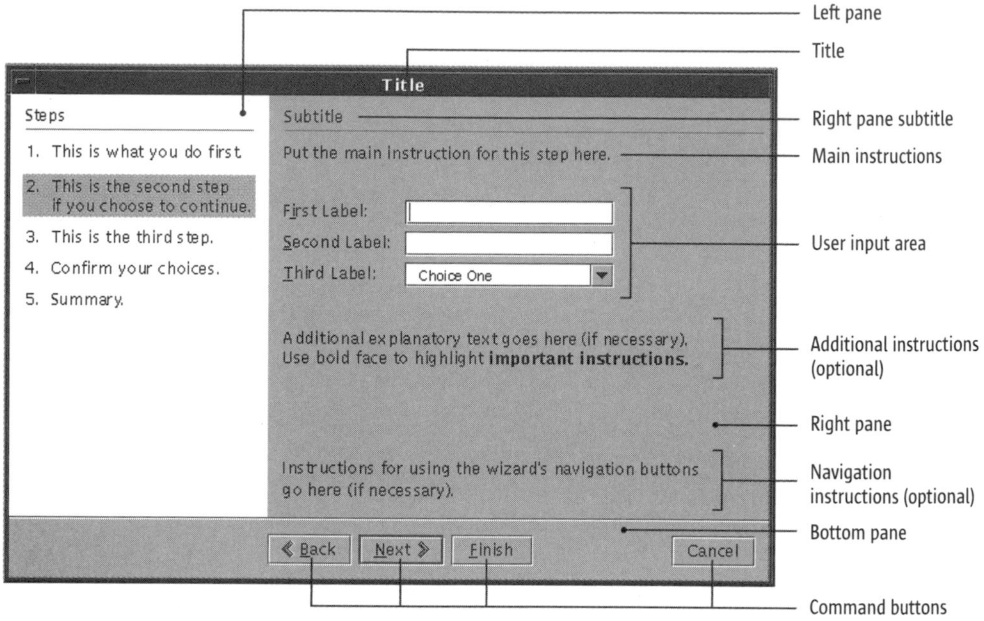

Each page consists of a title bar and three panes—right, left, and bottom—as shown in Figure 67.

- Title bar—Displays the wizard's title.
- Right pane—Typically contains user instructions and input fields for the current step. Alternatively, the right pane can contain explanations about the wizard, for example, an overview, operational feedback, or a summary of results.
- Left pane—Contains one of the following items:
    - A list of the wizard's steps
    - Help text about the object that has keyboard focus in the right pane
    - A graphic (a list of steps or help text is preferable)
- Bottom pane—Contains command buttons for navigating through the wizard.

A wizard can have several types of pages—for example, pages for collecting user input and a page that summarizes results. Figure 68 lists these page types and shows their order in a typical wizard.

FIGURE 68   Typical Order of Page Types in a Wizard

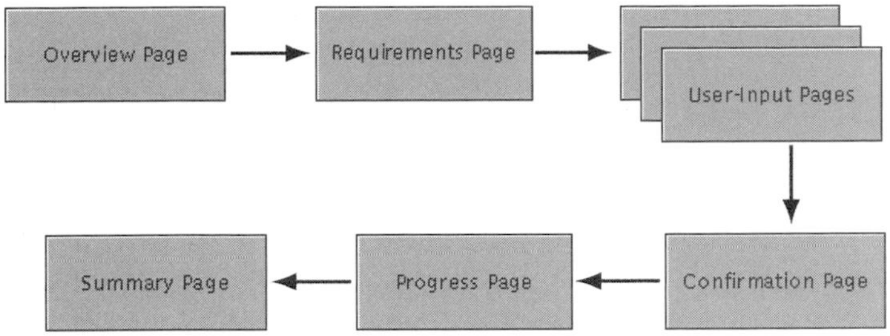

Only user-input pages are required in every wizard. Other page types are optional or are required only under certain conditions, explained in "Types of Wizard Pages" on page 116.

Standalone Wizards and Embedded Wizards   Wizards can be classified into two types—standalone and embedded—based on how users start them. A wizard that users can start directly—for example, from a desktop icon, a command line, or a file viewer—is called **standalone wizard**. A wizard that users can start only from within an application is called an **embedded wizard**, because it is embedded in that application. Typically, users start embedded wizards by choosing a menu item. Except where noted, guidelines in this chapter apply to standalone wizards and embedded wizards alike.

Typical Uses of Wizards   Although wizards vary widely in their purpose, most wizards are intended for one of the following purposes:

- Installing software
- Entering large amounts of related data
- Creating complex objects
- Performing complex procedures

Installing Software   The most common use of wizards is to install software. Such wizards—called **installation wizards**—collect data from a user and then install software accordingly. A typical installation wizard might set values in the operating system of a user's computer, move data from a CD-ROM to a hard disk, and configure the software being installed. Installation wizards are used by both computer novices and experienced users. (For more information about installation wizards, see "Designing Installation Wizards" on page 144.)

Entering Large Amounts of Related Data   An example of this type of task is setting up a new user account. Even if an application includes a dialog box for setting up user accounts, users who rarely perform this task might prefer to use a wizard, which divides a task into steps and explains each step. In contrast, system managers who set up new user accounts often probably would not use a wizard for that task.

Creating Complex Objects   In many applications, users can create and customize complex objects, such as charts, by choosing a series of menu items to create the object and then choosing more menu items to set the object's properties. New users, however, do not know which properties to set or in which order to set them.

Wizards help new users by:

- Presenting all the properties that a user needs to set
- Leading the user through setting each one

Typically, experienced users do not need such help.

Performing Complex Procedures   Many wizards perform complex procedures for users. For example, using options and parameter values that a user supplies, a wizard could create source code for an application that the user is writing. Typically, such wizards save users time and effort over other ways of performing the same task. For this reason, wizards that perform complex procedures are used by both computer novices and experienced users.

Deciding Whether You Need a Wizard   Although wizards can simplify and expedite many kinds of tasks, creating a wizard is not always the best solution for such tasks. To decide whether creating a wizard is appropriate for a particular task, answer the following questions:

- **How complex is the task?**

  Simple tasks seldom require wizards. Users can perform such tasks just as easily, if not more easily, with other kinds of user interfaces. For example, users might perform a simple task more quickly with a dialog box than with a three-page wizard.

  Consider providing a wizard for a task if the task is at least moderately complex.

- **Is the task performed by new users? Is the task performed rarely?**

  If you answered "yes" to either question, then providing a wizard might be appropriate.

Even technically sophisticated users should be considered new users if they are unfamiliar with your application or with its subject area—for example, accounting.

■ **Is the task usually performed in a fixed order?**

If so, consider implementing a wizard. If not—for example, if users need to organize data in different ways—consider another kind of user interface for the task.

■ **Is the application automating a significant part of the task?**

Wizards are most useful when they automate most of a user's task. For example, after asking a software developer just a few questions, a wizard might create more than 1,000 lines of customized source code for the developer's current project.

■ **Can you design a more direct or more efficient way for users to perform this task?**

Wizards are not always the best user interface for experienced users. Such users dislike answering questions that seem irrelevant to the task. If you provide a wizard for a task within an application, also provide alternative ways to perform the same task, unless the wizard automates a significant part of the task—as when installing software or creating complex objects.

A well-designed wizard helps users perform a task step-by-step and enables them to customize how the wizard performs the task. If a task needs a wizard, find out which parts of that task most users will perform. Then, design the wizard to meet the needs of those users. Omit rarely needed steps if you can provide another way to perform those steps.

Providing Alternatives to Wizards   Well-designed applications
provide more than one way to accomplish frequently performed tasks. Although wizards are an excellent user interface for the new or infrequent user, they can sometimes be too slow for the experienced user. In addition, because wizards are for only the most common steps of a task, they do not include unusual steps that experienced users might need.

In general, if you provide a wizard for a task, also provide other ways for experienced users to accomplish the same task. For example, if there is a command-line interface to your application, make it available in addition to your wizard. All the ways to perform a task must provide information that is accurate and mutually consistent.

Types of Wizard Pages   Wizards include two or more pages for
collecting a user's input and can include the following supplementary pages:

- Overview
- Requirements
- Confirmation
- Progress
- Summary

This section describes each type of wizard page. For information on laying out wizard pages, see "Designing Wizard Pages" on page 121. For information on designing the behavior of wizards, see "Designing Wizard Behavior" on page 138.

User-Input Pages   **User-input pages** enable users to customize how a wizard
performs its task. Each wizard has at least two user-input pages and can have as many such pages as are needed for the task. In general, it is better for a wizard to have several simple user-input pages than to have a few very complex ones.

Figure 69 shows a typical user-input page.

FIGURE 69   User-Input Page of a Wizard

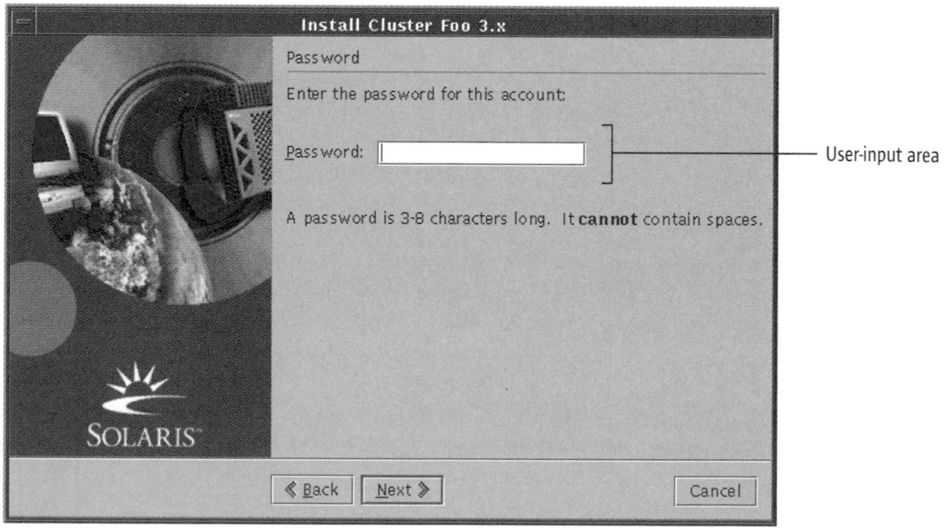

A wizard's usability depends on the usability of its user-input pages. The usability of those pages depends on the clarity of their text. The text should state:

- Which information the wizard needs from users
- How users should format the information
- What the wizard will do as a result of a user's responses

☕ Ensure that the text of user-input pages follows the conventions of good technical writing. Ask your team's technical writers or editors to help you write the text of your wizard's pages.

Overview Page

An **overview page** provides a brief introduction to the wizard and its steps. Typically, an overview page is needed only in very complex wizards or in wizards that do not display a list of steps in their pages. Figure 70 shows an overview page.

FIGURE 70   Overview Page of a Wizard

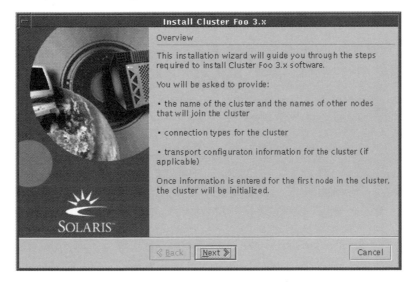

An overview page can help users determine whether a wizard meets their needs. In addition, an overview page can inform users about potential effects of using the wizard—for example, about either:

- The estimated duration of steps in the wizard
- Wizard operations that might significantly change a user's computer system

☕ Create an overview page as the first page of a wizard under any of the following conditions:

- The wizard is complex.
- The wizard's left pane does not display a list of steps.
- The wizard takes actions that might affect a user's system in unexpected ways.

Requirements Page   Some wizards have prerequisites that can make users abandon the wizard—typically, to gather more information or to perform additional tasks. Examples of such prerequisites are:

- Software that must be installed before starting the wizard
- A license number that must be entered before the wizard can complete its task

If your wizard will need information that a user might not have at the moment, notify the user by displaying a **requirements page** immediately after the overview page or as the first page of the wizard.

Figure 71 shows a requirements page.

FIGURE 71   Requirements Page of a Wizard

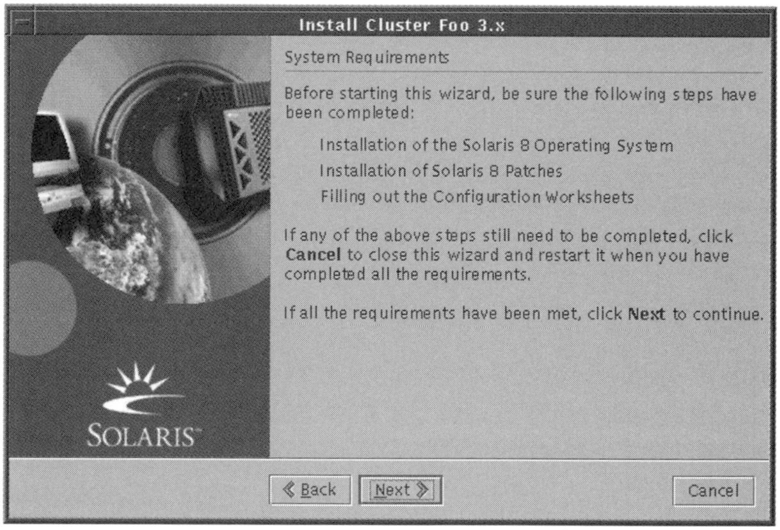

Make sure that users can view the requirements page before they begin to use your wizard. (For information relating to the requirements page of installation wizards, see "Helping Users Decide Whether to Install" on page 145.)

☕ If a wizard requires information or preconditions that might not be available when it starts, display a requirements page as the first page of the wizard or immediately after the overview page, if there is one.

Confirmation Page   A **confirmation page** shows all the data that the wizard has collected and provides information about the actions the wizard is about to take. Most wizards, except short ones, require a confirmation page.

Figure 72 shows a confirmation page.

FIGURE 72   Confirmation Page of a Wizard

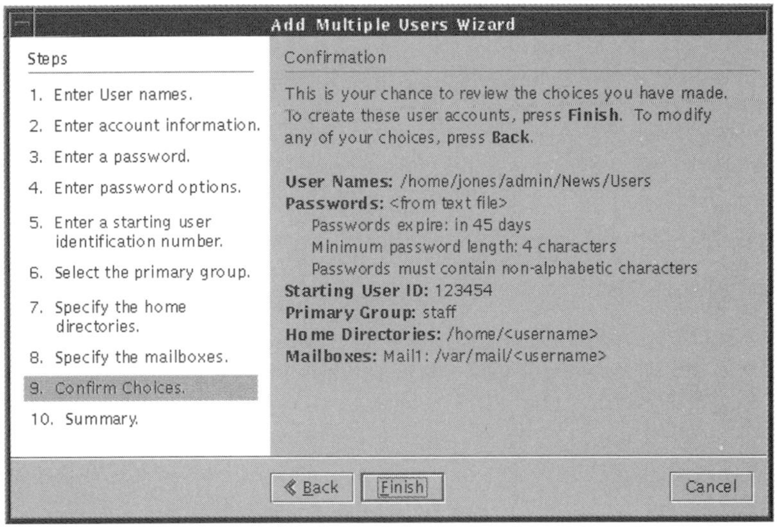

A confirmation page can contain information such as:

- A concise listing of the data that a user has entered in prior pages
- The set of actions that the wizard will perform upon leaving this page (beyond creating an object with the parameters specified by the user's data)
- How the wizard will modify a user's system
- Where the wizard will place items, such as in the installation directory
- The amount of disk space that the wizard's actions use and how much disk space will remain after the actions are complete
- An estimate of how long the wizard's actions will take

☕ Provide a confirmation page for all wizards with more than three pages of user input.

Progress Pages   A **progress page** provides feedback to users about the progress of a wizard's current operation. Figure 73 shows a typical progress page.

FIGURE 73   Progress Page of a Wizard

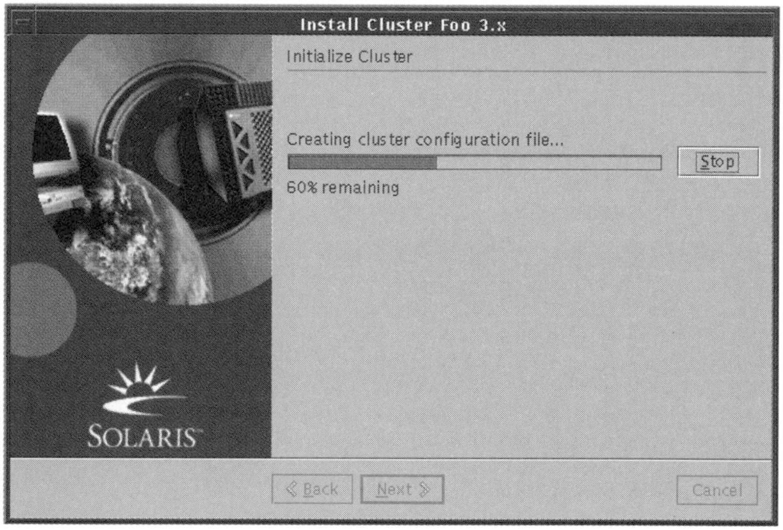

A progress page has the same basic layout as other types of wizard pages — for example, its right pane has a subtitle, and its bottom pane has navigation buttons. The right pane of a progress page also contains a progress bar or a progress checklist that reflects the state of the wizard's current operation.

In addition to providing feedback, a typical progress page enables users to stop the wizard's current operation by clicking the right pane's Stop button, as shown in Figure 73.

Clicking the right pane's Stop button is not equivalent to clicking the bottom pane's Cancel button (which cancels the wizard). On progress pages, the Cancel button is unavailable until a user clicks the Stop button. (For more information on the Cancel button, see "Designing the Bottom Pane" on page 124. For information on the Stop button in progress pages, see "Providing Operational Feedback in Wizards" on page 141.)

A wizard should display a progress page for each potentially time-consuming operation that the wizard performs. (For more information about providing feedback in wizards, see "Providing Operational Feedback in Wizards" on page 141.)

Summary Page   The **summary page** is an optional page that summarizes the work the wizard has performed and lists any actions users should take after closing the wizard. For example, the summary page can display an error log file, display a list of the files that have been updated, or explain how to access the software that has just been installed.

Figure 74 shows a summary page.

FIGURE 74   Summary Page of a Wizard

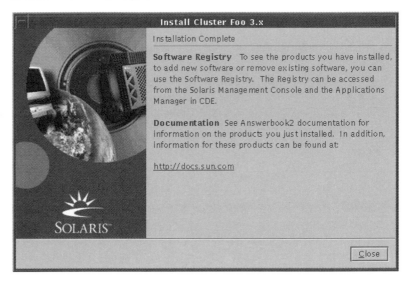

A summary page differs from a confirmation page. A confirmation page prepares users for the work that the wizard is about to perform and provides an opportunity for users to make changes. A summary page summarizes work that has been performed.

☕ Provide a summary page if a wizard has generated additional information that a user might want to examine after the task is completed.

Designing Wizard Pages   Each page of a wizard consists of four parts—a title bar and three panes, as described in "Fundamentals of Wizards" on page 111. Designing a page is a matter of designing each of its parts—choosing the right user interface elements for the page and then spacing them correctly.

Figure 75 shows the conventions for spacing and aligning the elements of wizard pages. Measurements in the figure are in pixels.

FIGURE 75   Spacing Conventions for Wizard Pages

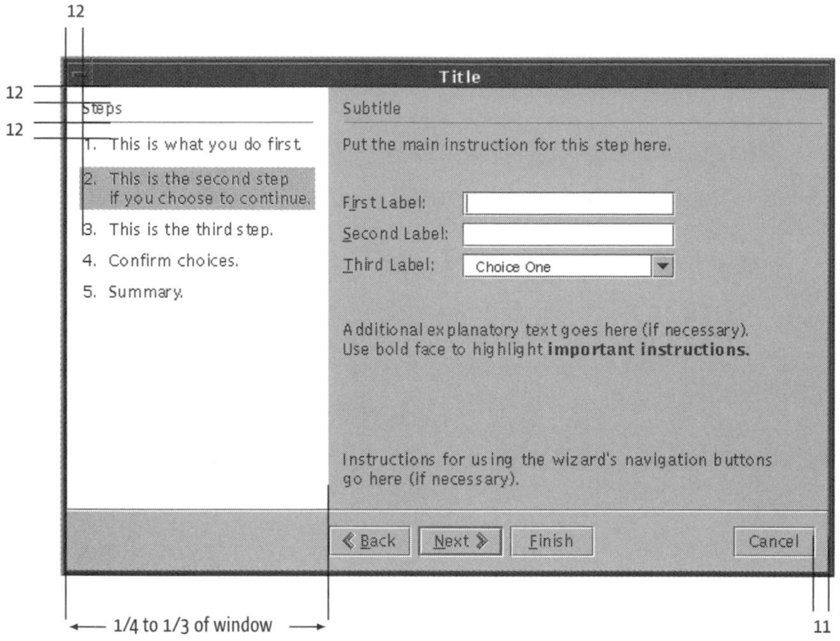

Spacing conventions are the same for all types of pages. (For a description of page types, see "Types of Wizard Pages" on page 116.) Wizard pages should also conform to the general conventions for spacing and alignment described in Chapter 4 of *Java Look and Feel Design Guidelines*, 2d ed.

☕ In each wizard page, include a title bar and three panes—left, right, and bottom.

☕ When designing wizard pages, follow the spacing conventions in Figure 75.

☕ In wizard pages, follow the spacing guidelines for dialog boxes, as specified in *Java Look and Feel Design Guidelines*, 2d ed., except when those guidelines are superseded by a more specific guideline for wizard pages.

☕ In the bottom pane of a wizard, align the left edge of the leftmost navigation button (the Back button) with the vertical line separating the left and right panes.

☕ In wizards, ensure that the left pane occupies one-fourth to one-third of the wizard's total width.

Designing the Title Bar   To design a wizard's title bar, you supply
descriptive title text in the correct format. Figure 76 shows title text in the
title bar of a typical wizard.

FIGURE 76   Title Text in the Title Bar of a Wizard

A wizard's title text should be the same on all pages; it should not include a
subtitle that changes from page to page. (The unique subtitle of each page
belongs in the right pane, as described in "Subtitles" on page 128.)

The correct format for a wizard's title text differs for standalone wizards and
embedded wizards. For embedded wizards, the format also differs depending
on whether the wizard's purpose is to modify an existing named object—for
example, an existing file named `MyConfiguration.txt`. The following
guidelines explain the correct format for title text in each type of wizard.

☕ Make an embedded wizard's title identical to the name of the
menu item for starting that wizard, unless the wizard's purpose is to modify
an existing named object. Do not end the title text with an ellipsis (...). You
can append the word "Wizard" to the title text—for example,
`New Chart Wizard` or `Configure Database Wizard`. However,
do not append the word "Wizard" to the name of the menu item.

☕ If an embedded wizard's purpose is to modify an existing named object,
format the wizard's title text like this: *Object Name - Command*.
(*Command* stands for the text of the menu command used to start the
wizard. The hyphen is preceded by one space character and followed by
another. Here is an example: `Firenze Cluster - Reconfigure`.)

☕ Use the following format for the title text of standalone wizards:
Wizard-Purpose Product-Name Product-Version, for example,
`Install Cluster Foo 3.0`.

Designing the Bottom Pane
The bottom pane of each wizard page displays a row of navigation buttons for moving between the wizard's pages and for closing the wizard. Different types of pages require different navigation buttons.

Figure 77 shows an example of navigation buttons for a wizard page.

FIGURE 77   Navigation Buttons in a Wizard

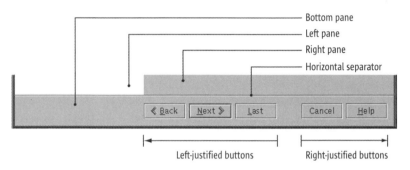

In Figure 77, notice the horizontal separator between the bottom pane and the two upper panes. The separator indicates that the bottom pane's navigation buttons relate to the entire wizard, not just to the contents of the current page.

The bottom pane can contain the following navigation buttons: Back, Next, Last, Cancel, Help, Finish, and Close. No single page contains all these buttons; the correct set of buttons depends on the type of the page.

Table 17 describes each navigation button that can be displayed in the bottom pane.

TABLE 17   Navigation Buttons for Wizards

Button Name	Description
Back	Displays the previous page. The Back button is present but unavailable on a wizard's first page and whenever a user cannot return to the previous page.
Next	Displays the next page.
Last	(Optional) Displays the wizard's final confirmation page. Include a Last button if users can skip subsequent pages by accepting the wizard's default values.
Cancel	Discards all user input and then closes the wizard without further processing. (The keyboard shortcut for the Cancel button is the Escape key.) On a progress page, the Cancel button is unavailable and dimmed unless the user halts the action in progress by clicking the Stop button in the right pane.
Help	(Optional) Displays help text outside the wizard window, using your application's online help system. Include the Help button only if your help text does not fit in the wizard's right or left pane.
Finish	Finishes all remaining parts of the wizard's task. Clicking the Finish button then either closes the wizard or displays the summary page, if there is one. Only the final confirmation page has a Finish button.
Close	Closes a wizard whose task is finished. Include the Close button only on a wizard's summary page (if any).

All wizard pages of the same type should display the same navigation buttons, in the same order.

Table 18 shows the correct order of navigation buttons for each page type.

TABLE 18   Order of Navigation Buttons in Wizard Pages

Page Type	Navigation Buttons
Overview page	
Requirements page	
User-input pages	
Confirmation page[1]	
	1. For a wizard without a Last button
Confirmation page[2]	
	2. For a wizard with a Last button
Progress page[3]	
	3. After a user presses the right pane's Stop button
Summary page	

In Table 18, notice that:

- Each page type has a default navigation button, which users can identify by its heavy border. (For more information about default buttons, see Chapter 10 of *Java Look and Feel Design Guidelines*, 2d ed.)

- Unavailable navigation buttons, if displayed, are dimmed. For example, the Back button is always dimmed on a wizard's first page, regardless of its page type.

■ Each button's mnemonic (if any) is underlined, and the mnemonic is the one recommended in *Java Look and Feel Design Guidelines*, 2d ed. (For more information on recommended mnemonics, see Appendix A in that book.)

☕ When designing the bottom pane of a wizard page, use the navigation buttons specified in Table 18. Order and format the buttons as specified in the table.

☕ Place a horizontal separator directly above the bottom pane in a wizard. In the bottom pane, align the left edge of the Back button with the left edge of the right pane. Right-justify the Cancel button and the Help button (if any).

☕ Make the Next button the default navigation button whenever it is available. Make the Next button unavailable until a user has entered all the required data for the page. (The default navigation button is also known as the default command button.)

☕ If feasible, provide a Last button in your wizard's bottom pane. A Last button enables users to skip pages with default values and complete the wizard more quickly.

Designing the Right Pane

The heart of a wizard page is its right pane, which can contain different kinds of information, depending on the type of the page. For example, on user-input pages, the right pane contains user-input areas and instructions for using them. On other pages, the right pane can display information such as an overview, operational feedback, or a summary of the wizard's results. Designing the right pane involves creating appropriate information and then laying it out correctly.

The guidelines in this section are mainly for user-input pages—the most important pages of a wizard. However, the topic "Subtitles" on page 128 applies to all wizard pages. For information about the right pane in progress pages, see "Providing Operational Feedback in Wizards" on page 141.

As shown in Figure 78, the right pane of user-input pages can contain the following parts:

■ Subtitle
■ Main instructions
■ User-input area
■ Additional instructions
■ Navigation instructions

FIGURE 78   Right Pane of a Typical User-Input Page

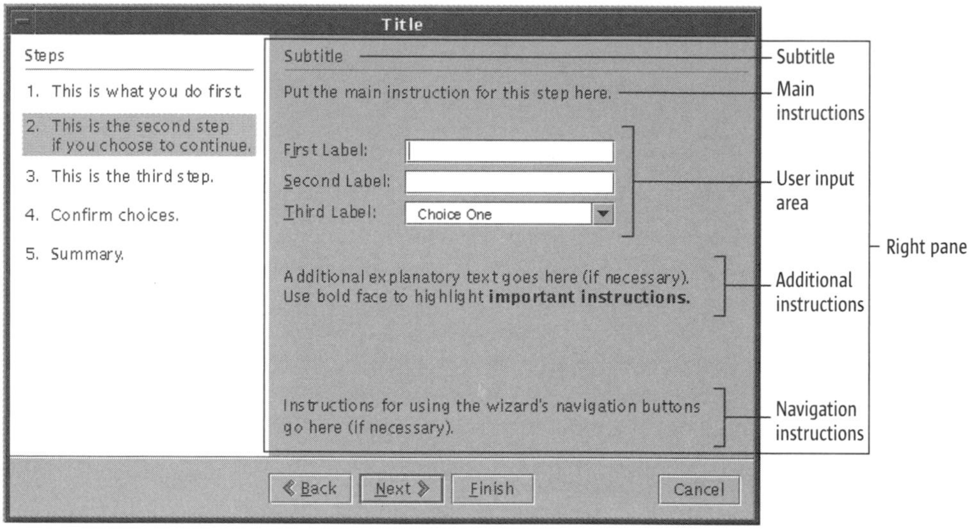

The rest of this section introduces each of these parts and describes how to design them.

Subtitles

In wizard pages, the right pane must have a subtitle that uniquely identifies the page and its purpose. Figure 78 shows the subtitle in a typical page.

☕ Ensure that the subtitle in a wizard's right pane identifies only the page displayed, not the entire wizard.

☕ Make the subtitle of each wizard page identical to the name of the wizard step to which the page belongs. (Typically, that name is listed in the left pane.) If the step has two or more pages, make each page's subtitle distinct by adding a page count—for example, (1 of 3)—or the suffix (Continued). Add a page count if you know the number of pages in the step.

☕ Place the subtitle of a wizard page at the top of the page's right pane. Use headline capitalization and left justification. (For a description of headline capitalization, see Chapter 4 of *Java Look and Feel Design Guidelines*, 2d ed.)

☕ Underline the subtitle of a wizard page with a rule whose width is 1 pixel and whose length equals that of the right pane, minus 12 pixels on the left and 6 pixels on the right. Display the rule in the color Secondary 2, as described in Chapter 4 of *Java Look and Feel Design Guidelines*, 2d ed.

☕ In a wizard's right pane, place a step number before the subtitle if the left pane contains no list of steps. Do not place a step number before the subtitle if the left pane contains a list of steps.

Main Instructions

Each user-input page displays main instructions that help users understand which information the page is requesting. Figure 78 shows a user-input page with main instructions.

On pages having only one user-input field, the main instructions can also serve as the label of that input field. On pages having two or more user-input fields, the main instructions must relate to all the fields. Each field must have its own label.

When writing the main instructions of a page, use imperative sentences—for example, "Enter your password." By using imperative sentences, which tell users what to do, you ensure that your wizard's requests for input are clear and concise.

☕ Place the main instructions of a wizard page directly below the underlined subtitle in the page's right pane, as shown in Figure 78.

☕ Write wizard instructions as imperative sentences.

☕ In wizard instructions, minimize the use of terms used solely for politeness—for example, "please" and "thank you."

User-Input Areas

Each user-input page has one or more user-input areas, as shown in Figure 78 on page 128. Each user-input area consists of a label and a control (such as a text box) that enables users to enter an input item (such as a user name).

Display a page's user-input areas directly below its main instructions. If a page has two or more user-input areas, they should request closely related input items—for example, a user's name and address.

If possible, provide a default value for each requested input item, such as a text entry or a radio-button setting. Verify that this value is valid and consistent with the user's choices so far. Ideally, the default value is the one that a typical user would choose.

Provide no default value for a requested input item if either:

- That item is optional, or
- No reasonable default value exists.

A data item is optional if a user can omit it without the wizard's supplying a default value.

No reasonable default exists if providing a default would confuse users. A
`user name` field, for example, has no reasonable default value, because
each user name must be unique. Instead of a default user name, you could
provide additional instructions explaining the required format for the user
name.

☕ In a wizard's user-input pages, place the user-input areas directly below
the main instructions.

☕ In wizards, place the word "Optional" to the right of each user-input
item that has no default value and that requires no input value from users.

☕ In wizards, provide a default value for each user-input value, unless no
reasonable default value exists. If you cannot supply a reasonable default
value for an item, ensure that the page's additional instructions explain the
valid formats for that item. In addition, request that input item early in the
wizard. Thus, you enable users to complete the wizard faster by skipping
pages that have default values for all user-input fields. (For more information
about enabling users to skip pages, see the description of the Last button in
"Designing the Bottom Pane" on page 124.)

☕ In wizard pages, ensure that the Next button is available only after
users enter all the data required on that page.

☕ Enable users to cut, copy, and paste between the wizard and text files,
and between the wizard and other opened applications. Use the keyboard
shortcuts specified in Appendix A of *Java Look and Feel Design Guidelines*,
2d ed.

☕ In wizard pages, ensure that a user's choices and changes remain
visible and in effect until the user cancels them. Users can cancel choices and
changes explicitly or by making subsequent conflicting choices on pages
visited later. Ensure that navigating back and forth through the wizard does
not cancel the user's choices and changes.

Additional Instructions   Optionally, the right pane of a page can have additional
instructions below its user-input areas. These additional instructions can
serve one or more of following purposes:

- To describe the correct format for entering input items
- To explain the meaning or consequences of choices that users make in the
  user-input area
- To explain command buttons or other controls displayed in the right pane

Figure 79 shows a page whose right pane contains additional instructions.

FIGURE 79   Additional Instructions in Wizard Page

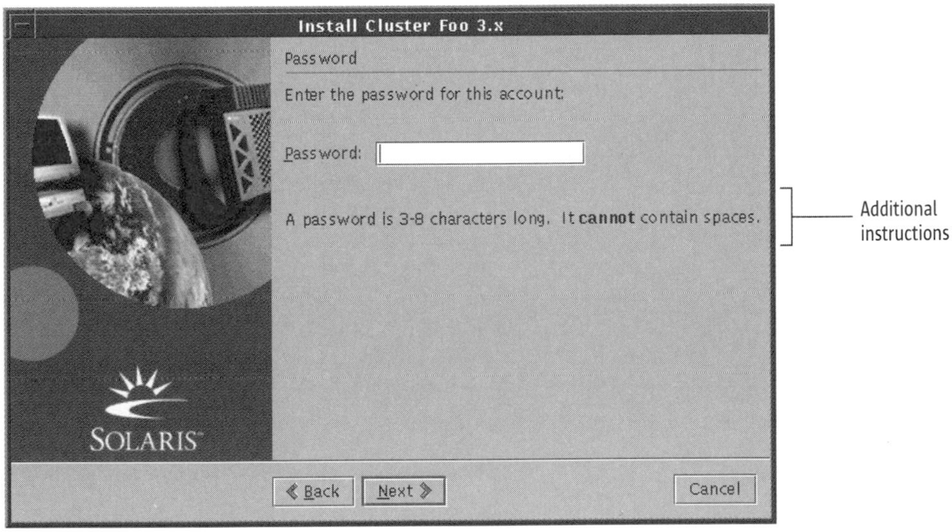

When laying out additional instructions, place them below the user-input area, so that experienced users can skip them.

In the additional instructions, you can use boldface type for text that you want to emphasize, but do not overuse it. If you need to provide additional text about an object displayed in the right pane, you can provide that text as help in your page's left pane.

☕ If a wizard page needs additional instructions, place them below the user-input area of the right pane.

☕ When describing how to perform an action in a wizard, state the outcome before stating the means to achieve it—for example, "To stop the print job, click Stop."

☕ If a wizard's additional instructions describe command buttons, use the following wording: "To *perform-this-action*, click *button-name*." For example, the instructions might be "To display more names, click More." Do not enclose the button name in quotation marks.

☕ In the additional instructions of a wizard page, warn users if completing the page will start actions that the wizard cannot completely undo.

Navigation Instructions   The bottom pane of a wizard contains navigation buttons for moving between pages and performing other general actions. If your wizard's users are unfamiliar with such buttons, you can place navigation instructions in the right pane of your wizard, as shown in Figure 78 on page 128. Do not provide navigation instructions if your wizard is intended only for experienced computer users.

☕ If a wizard will be used mainly by computer novices, provide instructions explaining each of the wizard's navigation buttons. Place these instructions only on the first page where each navigation button is displayed and available.

☕ When providing navigation instructions for a wizard, place them at the bottom of the right pane, directly above the wizard's navigation buttons, as shown in Figure 78.

☕ Use the following wording for instructions about navigation buttons: To *perform-this-action*, `click` *button-name*. Do not enclose the button name in quotation marks.

Designing the Left Pane   A wizard's left pane supplements the contents of the right pane by displaying one or more kinds of information — for example, a list of the wizard's steps. Within a particular wizard, the left pane always displays the same kind of information. For example, if the left pane of one page displays a list of steps, the left pane of each page displays a list of steps. Designing a wizard's left pane involves choosing the appropriate type of information to display and then laying it out correctly.

Deciding What to Display in the Left Pane   A wizard's left pane can display any one of the following items:

- A list of steps for using the wizard
- Help text about the object that has keyboard focus in the right pane
- Both a list of steps and help text
- A graphic (only if more-useful information is unavailable)

If possible, display steps and help text in the left pane of your wizard. A list of steps helps orient users within the wizard. Help text enables you to coach users without opening a help system outside the wizard.

If displaying steps and help text in the left pane is not practical, display either steps or help text in that pane. Display help text if you cannot list your wizard's steps — even its main steps. Display a list of steps if all your wizard's instructions are short and simple enough to fit in the right pane.

Left Pane with a List of Steps

If possible, use the left pane to list the steps that users need to follow in your wizard. Such a list helps users orient themselves within a wizard. Each step in the list can correspond to one or more wizard pages. Figure 80 shows a list of steps in the left pane of a typical page.

FIGURE 80   List of Steps in the Left Pane of a Wizard Page

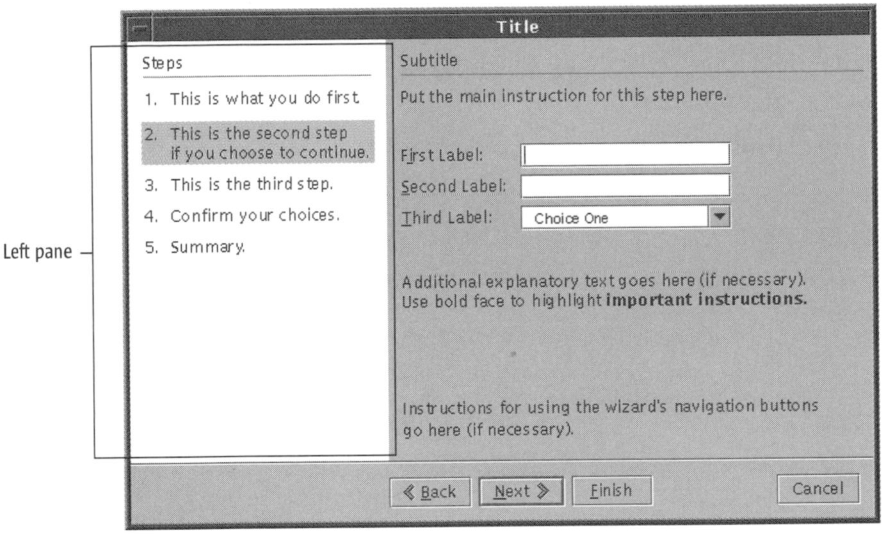

In a wizard's left pane, display a list of steps for using the wizard.

If the list of steps in a wizard's left pane is longer than the wizard page, display the list using a scroll pane with a vertical scrollbar. If resizing the wizard narrows the left pane, re-wrap the text of the list items to fit the narrowed pane. Do not provide a horizontal scrollbar.

If the left pane of a wizard page displays a list of steps in a scroll pane, make sure that each new step is visible in that list as users proceed through the wizard. When changing the view in the scroll pane, position the current step as the second one in the view, while displaying as many of the later steps as possible.

When displaying a list of steps in a wizard's left pane, highlight the current step, as shown in Figure 80. If a user navigates to a page in a different step, highlight the new current step and remove the highlight from the old one.

When highlighting the current step in a wizard's left pane, use the color Primary 3, as shown in Figure 80 and described in Chapter 4 of *Java Look and Feel Design Guidelines*, 2d ed. The highlight should be a rectangle as tall as the step and as wide as the left pane, minus ten pixels on the left and on the right. (This highlight differs from the normal one for text in the Java look and feel.)

☕ When defining the keyboard traversal order of a wizard page, omit the left pane. Instead, if there is a list of steps, use the text of the steps as the value for the page's accessible-description property. (For information about accessible descriptions, see Chapter 3 of *Java Look and Feel Design Guidelines*, 2d ed.)

Left Pane with Steps That Branch or Loop

In some wizards, the sequence of possible steps splits into two or more branches—for example, branches for typical and custom installations of software. Users of different branches need to perform different steps, which might not be consecutive in the sequence of possible steps. Displaying a list of steps in the left pane of such wizards requires careful planning.

If your wizard has branches, consider using one of the following techniques when designing the left pane:

- Display only your wizard's main steps, with each step corresponding to several pages if necessary. For example, combine several pages into a single step if you create several items of the same type.
- When a branch of your wizard skips several steps, move to the new current step and highlight that step in the list of steps.
- Change the list of steps dynamically, so that after a user chooses a step in a particular branch, only steps of that branch are displayed.

If none of these techniques would work for your wizard, omit the list of the steps from the left pane. In its place, display help text. (For more information, see "Left Pane with Help Text" on page 134.)

☕ Number the steps in the left pane of a wizard only if the steps are consecutive.

Left Pane with Help Text

If your wizard's instructions do not fit in the right pane, or if users might need assistance entering requested data, you can display help text in the left pane, as shown in Figure 81.

FIGURE 81   Left Pane with Help Text about a Field in the Right Pane

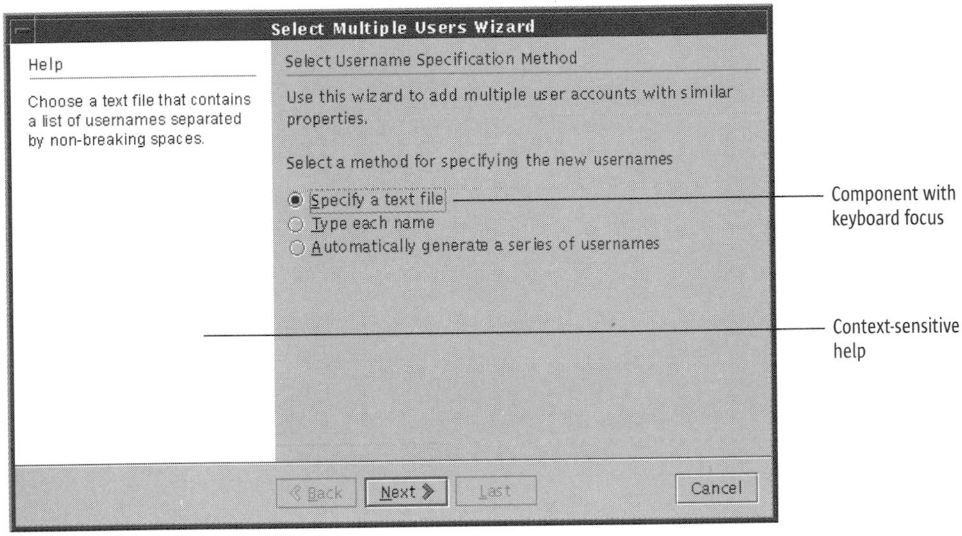

In the left pane of Figure 81, the help text describes the object that has keyboard focus in the right pane. If a user moves keyboard focus to a different object, the left pane displays help text about the object to which focus was moved.

Help text can be the sole contents of the left pane in wizards that do not list steps there.

☕ If you provide help text for any of your application's objects, provide help text for all the application's objects. Provide help on all your wizard's pages or on none.

☕ If a wizard's left pane displays help text, ensure that the help text describes a single object—the object that has keyboard focus in the right pane.

☕ If resizing a wizard narrows its left pane, re-wrap any help text to fit the narrowed pane. Do not provide a horizontal scrollbar.

Left Pane with Steps and Help Text   In wizards where the left pane displays both a list of steps and help text, you can use a pane having two tabs at the bottom, as shown in Figure 82.

FIGURE 82   Left Pane with Tabs for Steps and Help

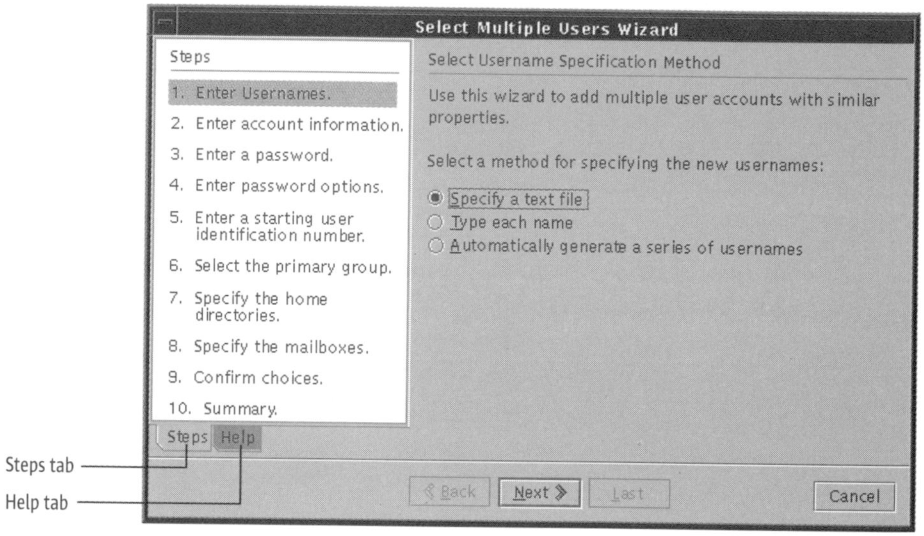

Steps tab ——

Help tab ——

When using the left pane to display both a list of steps and help text, follow the guidelines listed in "Left Pane with a List of Steps" on page 133 and in "Left Pane with Help Text" on page 134.

To display a list of steps and help text in the left pane of a wizard, use a pane having two tabs at the bottom. Label the tabs Steps and Help. Display the Steps tab unless a user clicks the Help tab.

Ensure that, if a user clicks a tab in a wizard's left pane, the tab's information is displayed until the user clicks the pane's other tab.

If a user clicks the Help tab of a wizard's left pane, display help text about the object that has (or most recently had) keyboard focus in the right pane.

Left Pane with a Graphic   Typically, the most useful information to display in a wizard's left pane is a list of steps or help text. Display a graphic in the left pane only if your wizard's steps are too complex to summarize in that pane and if there is no suitable help text. Figure 83 shows a graphic in the left pane of a page.

FIGURE 83   Graphic in Left Pane of a Wizard Page

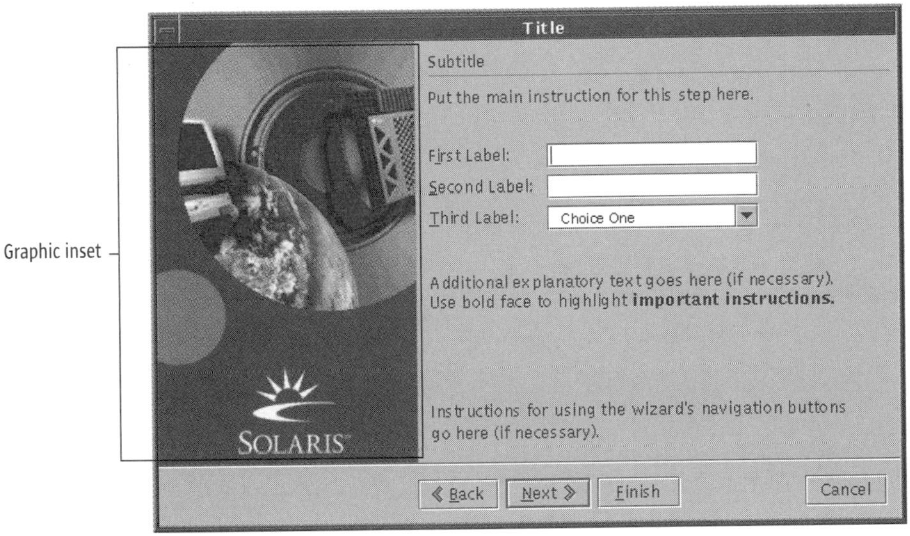

Graphic inset —

Ideally, graphics in the left pane relate to a user's task and to the current step of that task. For example, in a wizard that creates a complex object in several steps, the left pane might reflect a user's progress with a different graphic on each page. In a wizard that creates charts, the left pane might show an example pie chart if the user chooses an option labeled Pie Chart.

Do not resize the graphic if the left pane or the wizard is resized. Instead adjust the graphic as described in the following guidelines.

☕ Ensure that the dimensions of a graphic in a wizard's left pane are equal to the initial dimensions of that pane. Place the top of the graphic directly next to the wizard's title bar.

☕ Do not resize the graphic in a wizard's left pane if a user resizes that pane or the wizard. If the left pane becomes longer, fill its additional space with the background color of the graphic. If the wizard becomes narrower, reduce the width of the left and right panes proportionally, clipping the graphic as needed. If the wizard becomes wider, allocate the additional width to the right pane, after the left pane reaches its default size.

☕ If the left pane of your wizard's pages displays a graphic, provide information about the wizard's current step by changing the graphic on each page, if possible.

Designing Wizard Behavior
Just as important as a wizard's layout is its overall behavior:

- Is the wizard easy to start?
- Does it enable users to complete their entire task?
- Can it be moved and resized?
- Does it provide enough feedback?

This section discusses each of these topics.

Delivering and Starting Wizards
Some wizards are embedded in applications; others can be started directly. But whether the wizard is embedded or standalone, users must be able to find it and start it.

Most embedded wizards can be easily found and started, because they are started from menus or other obvious places within an application. Standalone wizards can be much harder to find and start—for example, wizards that install software from a CD-ROM or other removable storage medium.

On a CD-ROM, an installation wizard should be in an easy-to-find location. To simplify starting an installation wizard, consider creating an autoplay screen, which opens automatically when a user inserts the CD-ROM containing the wizard.

An **autoplay screen** lists the tasks that users can choose from the CD-ROM. If the only task is to install your software, the autoplay screen starts the first page of your installation wizard. If your users can use the CD-ROM for two or more tasks—such as installing software or viewing a Read Me file—precede your wizard's first page with a screen from which a user can choose from among the available tasks.

☕ Place an installation wizard at the highest level of a CD-ROM. If the application that the wizard will install is on a hard disk, place the wizard in the top-level directory for the application.

☕ Create an autoplay screen for a standalone wizard.

Supporting a User's Entire Task
When users begin a task in a wizard, they expect to complete the entire task before leaving the wizard. Make sure that your wizard enables users to perform their entire task without exiting or otherwise leaving the wizard. If the task requires temporarily closing the wizard—for example, to restart a user's computer—your wizard should reopen automatically at the correct wizard page.

If supporting a user's entire task is not possible, your wizard should tell the user which actions need to be performed outside the wizard. For example, if the user must temporarily exit the wizard to complete steps off line, the wizard should enable the user to print a list of those steps — including restarting the wizard.

When the user restarts the wizard, it should:

- Check that the user's computer system is in the required state
- Help the user correct any errors made during the offline steps

If your wizard cannot support a user's entire task, conduct a usability study. In the study, verify that all the participants can complete the entire task by using a combination of the wizard and steps performed outside the wizard.

Your wizard should enable users to perform follow-up actions that relate to the main task. For example, users often want to save information about the parameter values used in the wizard. Consider providing a way for users to print your wizard's confirmation page or to save its contents to a file. Also consider creating log files in a permanent location, so that users can have a record of the wizard's actions.

☕ Provide wizard support for the user's entire task.

☕ If technical constraints prevent your wizard from supporting a user's entire task, conduct a usability study to demonstrate that all participants can complete the task successfully.

Positioning and Sizing Wizards
Among the characteristics that affect a wizard's usability and visual appeal are:

- The screen position and size at which the wizard opens (and reopens)
- The wizard's appearance after resizing

Wizards are windows, so general guidelines for positioning them are discussed in "Setting the State of Windows and Objects" on page 28. This section supplements that discussion with information specifically about wizards.

A wizard must set its page size when opening for the first time. Typically, a wizard should be 400 pixels tall and 660 pixels wide. However, a wizard's size is determined by the **layout manager** used by the wizard's executable code.

If a user resizes a wizard, the resulting change in layout depends mostly on the wizard's layout manager. You need to specify how resizing should affect the contents of the wizard's left pane. The guidelines for resizing the left pane vary depending on whether it currently displays a list of steps, help text, or a graphic. (For more information, see "Designing the Left Pane" on page 132.)

☕ Open standalone wizards in the center of the screen on a user's principal video monitor.

☕ Open embedded wizards over their parent window—the primary window from which users invoke the wizard. (Position the wizard according to the guidelines in "Positioning Secondary Windows" on page 29.)

☕ If an embedded wizard's parent window contains information that must be visible while the wizard is displayed, ensure that the wizard leaves that information visible.

☕ When reopening a wizard after a user has closed it, display the wizard at the position it occupied when the user last closed it.

☕ If a wizard is resized horizontally, allocate any additional space to the left and right panes proportionally, unless the left pane contains a graphic. (For guidelines on resizing graphics in the left pane, see "Left Pane with a Graphic" on page 136.)

Checking Wizard Dependencies and User Input

A well-designed wizard does not start operations that it cannot finish. Before your wizard starts its task, it should verify that a user's computer system and software configuration meet all the wizard's requirements and dependencies. For example, the wizard should verify that the user's system has:

- Adequate disk space
- A compatible version of the operating system
- All required software patches
- All required Java technology classes, in the correct version

If possible, perform dependency checking at each wizard page, before the user moves to the next page. Some dependency checks can require information that the wizard collects across several pages. Perform such dependency checks as soon as possible and before the user moves to the wizard's confirmation page.

Before moving ahead from a page, your wizard should verify the user's input and alert the user to an any invalid values. To alert the user, your wizard should display an alert box. When the user closes the alert box, place keyboard focus on the first invalid item, and select that item automatically, if possible. Do not delete the user's input.

A validity check can take a long time. To let the user continue working, your wizard can delay displaying the results of the validity check until the check is complete. However, if the check finds invalid values, your wizard will have to recover from any errors caused by the user's invalid input.

☕ Provide dependency checking in your wizard to ensure that the wizard does not fail because of unsatisfied dependencies.

☕ In wizards, perform each dependency check as soon as possible after a user enters the relevant data. If a dependency does not involve user input, check it when the wizard first opens.

☕ Check all user input for errors before moving to a wizard's next page, unless checking would take an unreasonably long time. In that case, check for errors just before a user reaches the wizard's confirmation page.

Providing Operational Feedback in Wizards   Users interact more easily with a wizard if it keeps them informed about its state. Your wizard should display a progress page when performing a time-consuming operation. Figure 84 shows a typical progress page. (For a description of progress pages, see "Progress Pages" on page 120. For general information about appropriate response times, see Chapter 6.)

FIGURE 84   Progress Page with a Progress Bar

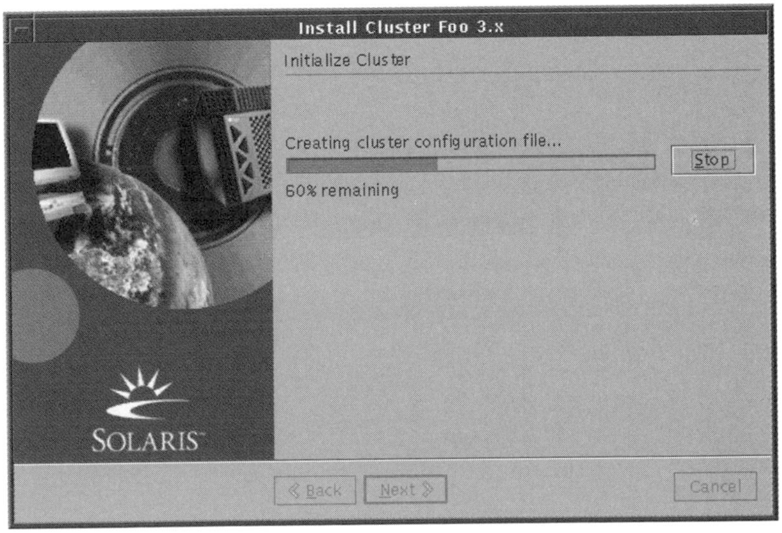

In a progress page, the right pane displays an underlined subtitle, formatted as on all other pages. Below the subtitle is a progress animation, which can be a progress bar (as in Figure 84) or a progress checklist (as in Figure 85).

FIGURE 85   Progress Page with a Progress Checklist

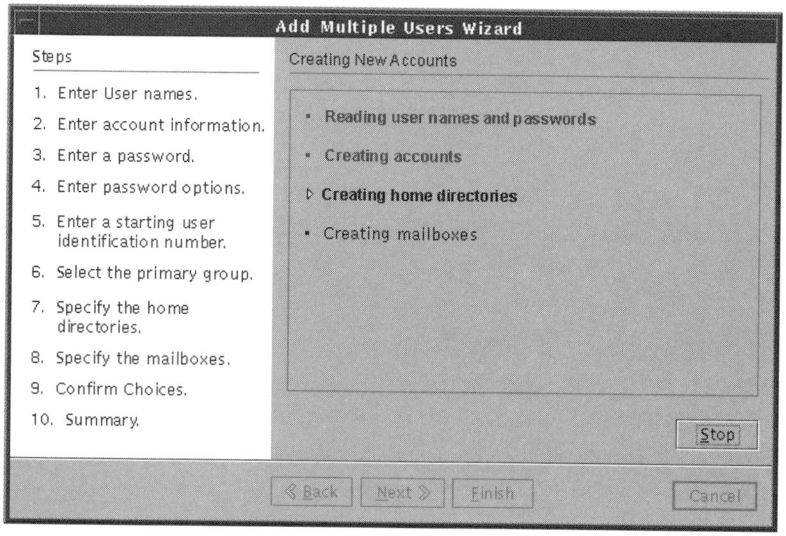

You can display a long progress checklist in a scrolling pane. A progress bar or progress checklist is displayed in the right pane, not in a separate window. (For general information about using progress bars and progress checklists, see "Providing Operational Feedback" on page 99.)

Applications should let users terminate an operation in progress. To let users terminate such an operation in your wizard, provide a Stop button on the progress page. Figure 84 and Figure 85 show a Stop button used with a progress bar and with a checklist. In both figures:

- The Stop button is right justified.
- The mnemonic for the Stop button is "S."
- The navigation buttons are dimmed (because the user has not clicked the Stop button).

Not all progress pages should have a Stop button. Before adding a Stop button to a progress page, consider whether terminating the operation could leave a user's computer system in an inconsistent state. If it could, decide whether your wizard can undo the completed portion of the operation.

Provide a Stop button only if your wizard can either:
- Undo the completed portion of operation, or

- Leave the user's computer system in a state less problematic than the one that would result from completing an incorrect action

Before stopping an operation, display an alert box explaining how stopping the operation will affect the task or the system—unless the system will be returned to its pre-wizard state. In the alert box, allow the user to continue the task or cancel the wizard.

☕ If a wizard performs an operation that might last longer than ten seconds, show progress feedback in the right pane of the wizard.

☕ If users can safely stop an operation in a wizard, provide a Stop button. Follow these rules:

- Place the Stop button directly below the progress bar or checklist on the progress page for the operation. Alternatively, place the Stop button directly to the right of the progress bar or checklist.
- Align the Stop button with the right edge of the page's content.
- Use "S" as the Stop button's mnemonic.

☕ If a user stops an operation, return the system to the state it was in when the operation started, or display an alert box that explains the state of the system when the operation stopped. The alert box must let the user choose whether to stop or continue the operation.

☕ On a progress page, make the navigation buttons of the bottom pane unavailable when an action is in progress. Unless the progress page is the wizard's final page, make the Next button available when the action is complete. Ensure that, after the action is complete, the Cancel button remains unavailable.

Alerting Users in Wizards   Ideally, a wizard's panes display all the text needed for using the wizard. You might need to alert users by displaying an additional text message—typically, about a potential or actual problem. You can alert users by displaying an alert box.

Display alert boxes only for errors that you cannot prevent. You can sometimes prevent errors by providing better instructions in the preceding wizard pages. Displaying alert box is required in the following situations:

- After the wizard detects an input error
- When a user is about to lose input data by canceling the wizard with either:
    - The window's close control, or
    - The wizard's Cancel button

Figure 86 shows an alert box for confirming a close-window operation.

FIGURE 86   Alert Box for Closing a Wizard

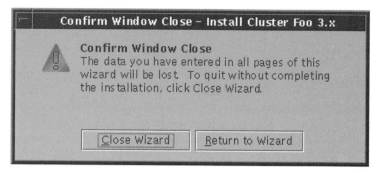

☕ Display a wizard's status information within the wizard's right pane. Display status information in an alert box only if you cannot display the information in the right pane.

☕ In wizards, display an alert box if a user provides input values but then tries to cancel the wizard by clicking its Cancel button or the close control in the wizard's title bar. In the alert box, display the message shown in Figure 86. If the user clicked the Cancel button, use the word "Cancel" instead of "Window Close" in the window title and message title.

☕ Ensure that a wizard warns users before it starts any operation that a user cannot stop. Typically, the warning is part of the additional instructions on the wizard page from which the user could request the operation.

Designing Installation Wizards
One of the tasks for which wizards are most frequently used is installing software. Although such installation wizards vary widely, all well-designed installation wizards share these characteristics:

- They are easy for users to locate and start.
- They provide all the information that users need to decide whether to install the software.
- They enable users to perform installation tasks completely, without exiting the wizard.

Choosing a Location for a Wizard's Code
The correct location for an installation wizard's executable code depends on whether the installation medium is portable—whether it is intended to be easily moved from one computer to another.

☕ If your installation wizard is intended to run from a portable medium, such as a CD-ROM, store the wizard at the highest-level directory of that medium.

☕ If your wizard is for installing an application whose installation files are on a hard disk, store the wizard at the highest-level directory of the application's installation files.

Helping Users Decide Whether to Install
Installation wizards should provide the following information to help users decide whether to proceed with an installation:

- The version of the software that the wizard installs and, if that version is not final and supported, a description such as Beta Release or Unsupported Release
- Pre-installation requirements, for example, the minimum hardware required
- Dependencies on other software that can affect the installation and later use of the software being installed
- Descriptions of the software modules available for installation
- The amount of disk space needed for the installation
- The location of a log file of actions taken during the installation
- A list of files that were modified or deleted by the installation

Tasks That Installation Wizards Should Handle
In addition to describing prerequisites, dependences, and results, installation wizards should enable users to perform the following tasks:

- Choose between a typical installation and a customized installation
- Install one or more modules of the software that can work independently of modules not installed
- Choose the directory in which the software will be installed
- Reinstall the software without losing data or application preferences

8: EVENTS AND ALARMS

Applications that monitor entities—such as variables, devices, or services—must keep users informed of events involving those entities. An **event** is a change in an application's state reflecting a change in the state of a **monitored entity**. An application or its users define which kinds of state changes are events. Some examples of events are:

- Starting a print job on a monitored printer
- Updating a monitored database
- Updating a variable that counts the bytes in a file

Most events do not require a user's attention. Such events are called **basic events**, which applications sometimes record in an **event log**.

Each event that might require a user's attention is called an **alarm event**. Applications display alarm events to users and record those events in an event log. The circumstances that caused an alarm event are called an **alarm**. The alarm event itself is also commonly called an alarm. Some examples of possible alarms are:

- The failure of a print job on a monitored printer
- An unsuccessful attempt to update a monitored database
- The growth of a monitored file beyond the maximum size allowed

Alarms vary in their severity, which can range from `minor` to `critical`, and in their status, which can progress from `open` to `fixed`. Each application or its users define which kinds of events cause alarms and how serious, or severe, each alarm is.

Applications that generate events should be able to:

- Record each alarm event in a log and inform users when a new alarm event occurs
- Display alarm views (representations of one or more alarms)
- Manipulate alarm views (for example, by sorting them at a user's request)

This chapter provides guidelines for designing your application's events and alarms.

Alarm Conditions

To determine when an application should create alarm events, the application's designer or users define **alarm conditions**, which when true, cause the application to create alarm events. Applications constantly monitor whether each alarm condition is true.

Each alarm condition defines either:

- A threshold on a monitored entity, or
- Thresholds on a set of monitored entities

A **threshold** is a value beyond which the alarm condition is true—or can be true, if the alarm condition depends on more than one threshold.

When true, an alarm condition constitutes an alarm on each monitored entity that the condition affects. A monitored entity for which an alarm condition is true is called an **alarmed entity**.

Levels of Severity

Each alarm event has a level of severity—known as the alarm's **severity**. An alarm's severity indicates the order in which users should handle that event relative to alarms of other severities.

Levels of severity can help an application's users prioritize their work, especially if the application can display many alarms at the same time. Table 19 lists the standard levels of severity for alarms.

TABLE 19   Levels of Alarm Severity

Severity	Description
Down	There is no response from the monitored entity (or from the device on which it resides).
Critical	An alarm condition occurred that seriously impairs service and requires immediate correction.
Major	An alarm condition occurred, impairing service but not seriously.
Minor	An alarm condition occurred that does not currently impair service, but the condition needs to be corrected before it becomes more severe.

Each level of severity has a corresponding **alarm graphic**, which you can use to help users identify alarmed entities. (For information about alarm graphics, see "Alarm Graphics" on page 150.)

Some applications can generate many alarms at the same time. To avoid overwhelming users, such applications should enable users to control:

- Which events trigger alarms
- Which level of severity is assigned to alarms

These capabilities help users eliminate irrelevant alarms and notice important alarms.

☕ Enable users to modify alarm conditions and define new alarm conditions.

☕ Provide only the levels of severity in Table 19. Of those levels, provide only the ones that your application's users will need.

☕ Enable users to adjust the thresholds that determine each alarm's severity.

☕ When displaying or logging an alarm, indicate its severity.

Alarm Status

Each alarm event has an **alarm status** that affects:

- Whether the application displays information about that event
- How the application displays that information

Table 20 describes the values for an alarm's status.

TABLE 20 Alarm Status Values

Status	Description
Open	This alarm event is neither `closed` nor `fixed` and is not being handled by another user.
Acknowledged	This alarm event is neither `closed` nor `fixed` and is being handled by the user who set the event's status to `acknowledged`.
Closed	Either the alarm condition associated with this alarm event is no longer true, or a user did something that canceled the alarm. (An alarm event's status can be `closed` even if nothing has corrected the problem that caused the event.)
Fixed	The problem that caused this alarm event has been corrected.

An alarm whose status is `open` or `acknowledged` is called an **active alarm**. An alarm whose status is `closed` or `fixed` is called an **inactive alarm**. Neither "active" nor "inactive" is an alarm status.

Logging Events
To enable users to examine a record of events, your application can display an event log—a complete or partial record of events. An application can have one event log or several. For example, an application might have a log for each monitored entity.

Make sure that users can easily find your application's event logs and manipulate their contents—with, for example, an operating system's utility program for sorting plain text.

☕ If users might need event-related information after your application no longer displays it, store that information in a persistent event log—for example, a text file.

☕ If your application has event logs, provide commands—within the application—for displaying each log's name and location. Likewise, provide commands for renaming and moving each log.

Displaying Alarm Views
An **alarm view** is a window or pane that displays representations of alarms. For example, an alarm view might represent alarms in one of the following forms:

- Badges on icons
- Badges on nodes in a tree
- Rows in a table

You can help users work with alarms more efficiently by providing different alarm views for different user tasks. Provide at least the following alarm views:

- **Monitored-entities view**—A tree or pane that displays an icon and an alarm graphic for one or more monitored entities and their containers. (For more information, see "Monitored-Entities View" on page 152.)
- **Detailed alarm view**—A table of all active and inactive alarms that match certain criteria—typically, alarms for a particular monitored entity. Each table row describes a particular alarm in detail. (For more information, see "Detailed Alarm View" on page 154.)

The rest of this section describes how to design alarm views, including how to use alarm graphics.

Alarm Graphics
An **alarm graphic** is an application graphic that indicates an alarm's existence and severity. Alarm graphics help users notice alarms and respond to them in the appropriate order.

You can use each alarm graphic as either:

- An alarm badge (a badge on an icon), or
- An alarm symbol (an alarm graphic displayed alone)

Figure 87 shows the same alarm graphic used as a badge and as a symbol.

FIGURE 87   Alarm Graphic Used as a Badge and as a Symbol

Table 21 shows a recommended set of alarm graphics and the level of severity that each graphic represents.

TABLE 21   Alarm Graphics for the Standard Levels of Severity

Severity	Graphic	Description
down	⊙	There is no response from the monitored entity (or from the device on which it resides).
critical	⊙	An alarm condition occurred that seriously impairs service and requires immediate correction.
major	⊘	An alarm condition occurred, impairing service but not seriously.
minor	⊖	An alarm condition occurred that does not currently impair service, but the condition needs to be corrected before it becomes more severe.

In alarm views, display an alarm graphic on each representation of an alarmed entity or of that entity's alarm events.

For example, display an alarm graphic:

- On the icon for each alarmed entity
- In each table row that describes an alarm event
- On the icon for each container that contains an alarmed entity

Display an alarm graphic wherever you refer to a collection of alarms having the same level of severity. For example, display the alarm graphic in headings and labels for such collections. Using alarm graphics in this way helps users associate each graphic with its meaning.

You can display alarm graphics in different sizes. The correct size for each alarm graphic depends on the view that displays the graphic.

If the alarm view is in an icon pane or a tree, place an alarm graphic as a badge on the lower right corner of the icon for each alarmed entity, as shown in Figure 88 (an icon pane) or Figure 89 (a tree). Use a small alarm graphic on small icons; use a larger alarm graphic on large icons.

If the alarm view is in a table, place an alarm graphic in each row of a column dedicated to alarm graphics, as shown in Figure 91 on page 155.

☕ In alarm views, place an alarm graphic on each representation of an alarmed entity.

☕ When displaying alarm graphics, use only the alarm graphics in Table 21.

☕ When placing an alarm graphic on icons, ensure that the alarm graphic covers no more than 25% of the icon.

☕ In the standard locations for alarm graphics, display only alarm graphics. Never display any other information in those locations. If an entity is not alarmed, indicate that fact by displaying nothing in the standard locations for alarm graphics.

☕ When representing a monitored entity where more than one alarm exists, display an alarm graphic only for the entity's most severe alarm.

☕ When representing a container that contains alarmed entities, display only one alarm graphic—the graphic for the most severe alarm among those for the container's contents. If the container has other containers, consider the contents of the entire hierarchy when determining which graphic to display.

Monitored-Entities View   A monitored-entities view displays an icon and alarm graphic for one or more monitored entities or containers of such entities. Figure 88 shows a monitored-entities view as an icon pane.

FIGURE 88   Monitored-Entities View as an Icon Pane

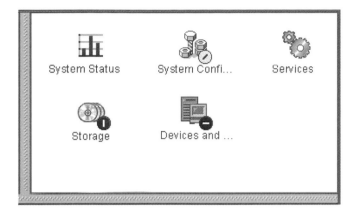

Figure 89 shows a monitored-entities view as a tree.

FIGURE 89   Monitored-Entities View as a Tree

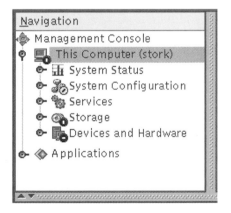

A monitored-entities view enables users to determine:

- Whether any alarmed entities are in that view
- How severely each entity is alarmed

When examining monitored-entities views, users might need more information about a particular entity. You can provide that information through supplements such as:

- Tool tips for the entities in the view
- Context-sensitive help in an additional pane of the window containing the monitored-entities view

Figure 90 shows a monitored-entities view with tool tips.

FIGURE 90   Monitored-Entities View with Tool Tips

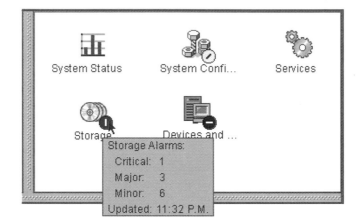

In each tool tip, help pane, or other supplement to a monitored-entities view, display:

- The name of the monitored entity
- The time at which the entity's status was most recently updated
- Brief information about the entity

☕ Supplement each monitored-entities view with at least one form of additional information about each entity in the view. For example, provide tool tips, context-sensitive help, or both.

Detailed Alarm View   A **detailed alarm view**, or "detailed view," is a table of all active and inactive alarm events that match certain criteria, defined by an application's designer or by a user. Each table row provides detailed information about a particular alarm event. Figure 91 shows a detailed alarm view.

FIGURE 91   Detailed Alarm View

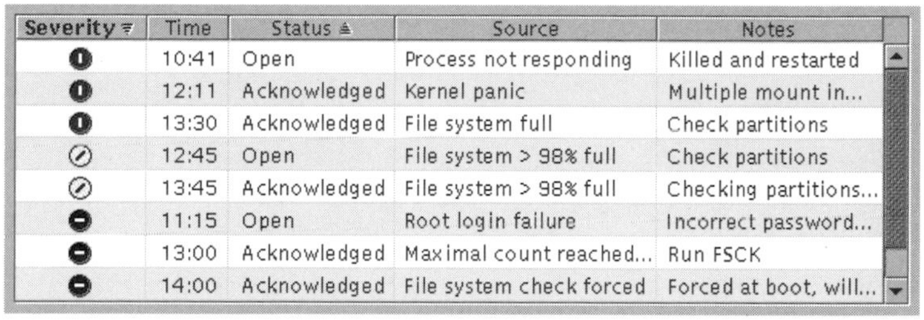

Severity ⩒	Time	Status ⩘	Source	Notes
❶	10:41	Open	Process not responding	Killed and restarted
❶	12:11	Acknowledged	Kernel panic	Multiple mount in...
❶	13:30	Acknowledged	File system full	Check partitions
⊘	12:45	Open	File system > 98% full	Check partitions
⊘	13:45	Acknowledged	File system > 98% full	Checking partitions...
⊖	11:15	Open	Root login failure	Incorrect password...
⊖	13:00	Acknowledged	Maximal count reached...	Run FSCK
⊖	14:00	Acknowledged	File system check forced	Forced at boot, will...

The kinds of detailed views that you should provide depend on the tasks that your application's users need to perform. For each monitored entity provide at least one detailed view that displays all alarms for that entity.

For each alarm in a detailed view, display:

- Alarm's level of severity
- Time at which the alarm occurred
- Status of the alarm event
- Alarm condition that caused the alarm
- Notes that users have entered about the alarm

For each detailed view, enable users to manipulate the displayed alarms. For example, enable users to:

- Sort alarms
- Filter alarms
- Delete an alarm
- Undo the deletion of an alarm
- Change an alarm's status—for example, by acknowledging or closing the alarm
- Add notes about an alarm

☕ In a detailed alarm view, enable users to request information about each active and inactive alarm for the monitored entities in that view.

☕ When displaying alarms in a detailed view, show the severity of each alarm.

☕ In detailed alarm views, enable users to sort and filter alarms by their status, level of severity, time of occurrence, and optionally, other criteria.

☕ In a detailed alarm view, display only alarms that match a user's criteria, or by default, display only active alarms. By default, when displaying alarms, sort them primarily by their severity (listing the most severe alarm first). In addition, sort the alarms secondarily by their alarm status (listing open alarms first).

If a detailed alarm view is filtered by default or at a user's request, clearly indicate that the view is filtered and by which criteria.

GLOSSARY

accessibility
The degree to which software can be used comfortably by a variety of people, including those who require assistive technologies or those who use the keyboard instead of a pointing device. An accessible JFC application uses the Java Accessibility API and provides keyboard operations for all actions that can be carried out by use of the mouse.

action window
A dialog box that prompts a user for information needed to perform an action the user requested—for example, opening a file.

activation
Starting the operation of a component. See also **available**, **choose**, **select**.

active alarm
An alarm whose status is `open` or `acknowledged`. See also **alarm event**.

Add-and-Remove idiom
Enables users to choose a subset from a large list of objects. See also **idiom**.

alarm
See **alarm event**.

alarm condition
A condition that, when true, causes an application to create an alarm event.

alarm event
In a user interface with events and alarms, an event that might require a user's attention. The set of circumstances that cause an alarm event is called an alarm. The alarm event itself is also commonly called an alarm. See also **event**, **basic events**.

alarm graphic
An application graphic that indicates an alarm's existence and severity.

alarm status
For an alarm event, a property that affects whether an application displays information about that alarm event and, if so, how.

alarm view	A window or pane that represents alarms as, for example, badges on icons, rows in a table, or nodes of a tree.
alarmed entity	A monitored entity for which an alarm condition is true. See also **monitored entity**.
alert box	A secondary window used by an application to convey a message or warning or to gather a small amount of information from the user. Four standard alert boxes (Info, Warning, Error, and Question) are supplied for JFC applications. Alert boxes are created using the `JOptionPane` component. See also **dialog box**.
application	A program that combines all the functions necessary for a user to accomplish a particular set of tasks (for example, word processing or inventory tracking). Unless stated otherwise, this book uses "application" to refer to both applets and standalone applications.
application-provided table	A table whose structure is provided by the application, though users might be able to select or edit the table's contents. Application-provided tables differ from user-created tables, such as spreadsheets, whose structure is determined by a user.
application-wide mode	Changes the effect of users' actions throughout the application. Examples of application-wide modes are the Edit mode and Run mode of a typical GUI builder. See also **mode**.
ascending sort	A sort in which values are arranged from lowest to highest.
automatic row sorting	In tables, a feature that causes rows to be automatically sorted each time users edit a row or add one.
available	Able to be interacted with. When a component is unavailable, it is dimmed and is unable to receive keyboard focus.
backing window	A container, a sort of "virtual desktop," for an MDI application. See also **internal window**, **MDI**.

badge
A graphic added to an existing graphic to provide additional information about that existing graphic—for example, to indicate a change in the action that a button represents or to indicate the presence of a problem in the entity that an icon represents.

basic events
In a user interface with events and alarms, events that do not require a user's attention. See also **alarm event**.

behavior
Refers to how applications interact with users. See also **mode**, **tool tip**, **filtering**, **searching**.

benchmark
A goal that you devise to determine whether your application provides acceptable response delays for a specific task. See also **response delay**.

bounding box
In icon panes and other two-dimensional layouts, the expanding rectangle that marks the starting position and current position of the pointer as a user drags the mouse.

Browse idiom
Enables users to specify an object (typically, a file, directory, or web page) by choosing it from a list. This idiom consists of a label, an editable text field, and a command button whose text begins with the word "Browse." See also **idiom**.

cell-selection model
A selection model in which users of a table can select a single cell without selecting that cell's entire row. See also **row-selection model**, **selection model**.

cell-selection table
A table which users can select a single cell without selecting its entire row.

checkbox
A control, consisting of a graphic and associated text, that a user clicks to turn an option on or off. A check mark in the checkbox graphic indicates that the option is turned on. Checkboxes are created using the JCheckBox component.

choose
(1) In human interface design, refers narrowly to turning on a value in a component that offers a set of possible values, such as a combo box or a list box.

(2) In technical documentation, refers generally to the action of clicking a menu title or menu item. See also **activation**, **select**.

click   To press and release a mouse button. Clicking selects or
                        activates the object beneath the button.

client   In the client-server model of communications, a process that
                        requests the resources of a remote server, such as
                        computation and storage space. See also **server**.

combo box   A component with a drop-down arrow that the user clicks to
                        display a list of options. Noneditable combo boxes have a
                        list from which the user can choose one item. Editable
                        combo boxes offer a text field as well as a list of options.
                        The user can make a choice by typing a value in the text
                        field or by choosing an item from the list. Combo boxes are
                        created using the `JComboBox` component.

command button   A button with a rectangular border that contains text, a
                        graphic, or both. A user clicks a command button to specify
                        a command to initiate an action. Command buttons are
                        created using the `JButton` component. See also
                        toggle button, **toolbar button**.

common menu   Any one of the drop-down menus present in most menu-
                        driven applications. The common menus are the File menu,
                        Edit menu, View menu, and Help menu.

component   A subclass of `java.awt.component` or, by extension, the
                        interface element implemented by that subclass. Most
                        components—for example, menus and toolbars—enable a
                        user to control an application.

**computational
performance**   What software engineers usually mean by "performance"—
                        focuses on fast algorithms, efficient data structures, and
                        economical use of processor time.

confirmation page   In wizards, a type of page that enables users to verify which
                        actions a wizard is about to take and then start or cancel
                        those actions.

container   A component (such as an applet, window, pane, or internal
                        window) that holds other components.

Container-and-Contents idiom Allows users to view a hierarchy of containers—for example, a set of file folders—while also viewing the contents of a selected container—for example, the list of documents in a selected folder. See also **idiom**.

contextual menu A menu displayed when a user presses mouse button 2 while the pointer is over an object or area associated with that menu. A contextual menu offers only menu items that are applicable to the object or region at the location of the pointer. Contextual menus are created using the `JPopupMenu` component. See also **menu**.

control An interface element that a user can manipulate to perform an action, choose an option, or set a value. Examples include buttons, sliders, list boxes, and combo boxes. See also **component**, **object**.

cross-platform Pertaining to heterogeneous computing environments. For example, a cross-platform application is one that has a single code base for multiple operating systems.

cursor See **pointer**.

dedicated property window Affects only objects that were already selected when the property window opened. The window affects the same objects even if a user changes the selection while the property window is displayed. See also **property window**.

default command For an object, the command that is executed if a user double-clicks that object. See also **object**.

default command button The command button that the application activates if a user presses Enter or Return. Default buttons in Java look and feel applications have a heavier border than other command buttons. See also **command button**.

deployment The process of installing software into an operational environment.

descending sort A sort in which values are arranged from highest to lowest.

designer   A professional who specifies how users will interact with an application, chooses the application's user-interface components, and lays them out in a set of views. The designer might also be the developer who writes the application code.

detailed alarm view   A table of all active and inactive alarm events that match certain criteria, defined by an application or by a user. (Also called "detailed view.")

dialog box   A secondary window displayed by an application to gather information from users. Examples of dialog boxes include windows that set properties of objects, set parameters for commands, and set preferences for use of the application. Dialog boxes can also present information, such as displaying a progress bar. A dialog box can contain panes, lists, buttons, and other components. Dialog boxes are created using the JDialog component. See also **action window**, **alert box**, **property window**, **secondary window**, **utility window**.

drop-down arrow   The triangular indicator that a user clicks to view more options than are visible on screen—such as the list attached to a combo box or the menu provided by some toolbar buttons. See also **badge**.

drop-down menu   A menu that is displayed when a user activates a menu title in the menu bar or toolbar. Drop-down menus are created using the JMenu component. See also **menu**, **menu bar**.

duration   For tool tips, the amount of time for which a tool tip is displayed. See also **onset delay**, **tool tip**.

editing area   In tables using the row selection model and the external editing model, an area outside the table and, typically, just below it. The editing area includes editable text fields, combo boxes, or other editable components that enable users to type or choose input values. See also **editing model**, **external editing model**, **row-selection model**.

editing model   In a table, a set of rules and techniques for editing a portion of the table, such as a cell or row. See also **selection model**.

ellipsis (...)	At the end of a menu item, indicates that an application needs additional user input to execute the item's command. An ellipsis indicates that the application will display a dialog box before the command is executed.
embedded wizard	A wizard that users can start only from within an application. See also **wizard**, **standalone wizard**.
event	A change in an application's state reflecting a state change in an entity that the application monitors. See also **alarm event**, **monitored entity**.
event log	A complete or partial record of events.
external editing model	In tables, a technique of editing the contents by entering values in an editing area located outside the table. See also **internal editing model**.
external progress animation	An animation that indicates progress feedback but not in a dedicated area for indicating the progress or status of operations. See also **internal progress animation**.
filtering	In user interfaces, a feature that enables users to specify which objects in a currently displayed set should be omitted from the display, based on the user's criteria, known as a filter.
focus	See **keyboard focus**.
glyph	A small graphical symbol.
golden mean	A position on a window's vertical midline and slightly above the window's horizontal midline.
grid line	In tables, a horizontal or vertical line separating rows or cells.
host	A computer system that is accessed by one or more computers and workstations at remote locations.
icon	An on-screen graphic representing an interface element that a user can select or manipulate—for example, an application, document, or disk.
icon pane	A set of icons in a pane. See also **icon**, **pane**.

idiom

A set of components configured in a standardized way to provide a particular appearance and behavior.

import

To bring an object or data file (for example, a document created in another application, a text file, or a graphics file) into an application.

inactive alarm

An alarm whose status is `closed` or `fixed`. See also **active alarm**, **alarm event**.

indeterminate-progress bar

Used to provide feedback about an operation whose duration you cannot estimate and whose sequence of stages you cannot represent. See also **progress bar**.

input focus

See **keyboard focus**.

insertion point

The place, usually indicated by a blinking bar, where typed text or a dragged or pasted selection will appear. See also **pointer**.

inspecting property window

Displays a continuously updated view of the property values for the selected object, and enables a user to change the displayed property values (and the selected object) immediately. See also **property window**.

installation wizard

A wizard that installs software.

internal editing model

In tables, a technique of editing the contents by entering a value directly in the cell that has focus. See also **external editing model**.

internal progress animation

An animation in an application's dedicated area for indicating the progress or status of operations. See also **external progress animation**.

internal window

In MDI applications, a window that a user cannot drag outside the backing window. In an MDI application that uses the Java look and feel, internal windows have a window border, title bar, and standard window controls with the Java look and feel. Internal windows correspond to a non-MDI application's primary windows. See also **backing window**, **MDI**, **primary window**.

Java Accessibility API   A programming interface (part of the JFC) that enables assistive technologies to interact and communicate with JFC components. A Java application that fully supports the Java Accessibility API is compatible with such technologies as screen readers and screen magnifiers.

Java Foundation Classes   See **JFC**.

Java look and feel   The default appearance and behavior for JFC applications, designed for cross-platform use. The Java look and feel works in the same way on any platform that supports the JFC.

JFC   (Java Foundation Classes) A part of the Java 2 platform that includes the Swing classes, pluggable look and feel designs, and the Java Accessibility API. The JFC also includes the Java 2D API, drag and drop, and other enhancements.

JFC application   An application built with the JFC. See also **JFC**.

keyboard focus   The active window or component where the user's next keystrokes will take effect. Sometimes called the "input focus." See also **select**.

keyboard operations   A collective term for keyboard shortcuts, mnemonics, and other forms of navigation and activation that utilize the keyboard instead of the mouse. See also **keyboard shortcut**, **mnemonic**.

keyboard shortcut   A keystroke combination (usually a modifier key and a character key, like Control-C) that activates a menu item from the keyboard even if the relevant menu is not currently displayed. See also **keyboard operations, mnemonic**.

keyboard traversal order   The sequence of fields that will receive keyboard focus if a user repeatedly presses the Tab key. See also **keyboard focus**.

Key-Search idiom   A feature that lets users find a list item by typing its first letter (called the "search key" or "key"). Key search is case insensitive, and it works on any list of text items, even an unsorted list. See also **idiom**.

label   Static text that appears in the interface. For example, a label
                           might identify a group of checkboxes. (The text that
                           accompanies each checkbox within the group, however, is
                           specified in the individual checkbox component and is
                           therefore not considered a label.) Labels are created using
                           the `JLabel` component.

layout manager   Software that assists the designer in determining the size
                           and position of components within a container. Each
                           container type has a default layout manager.

list box   A set of choices from which a user can choose one or more
                           items. Items in a list can be text, graphics, or both. List
                           boxes can be used as an alternative to radio buttons and
                           checkboxes. The choices that users make last as long as the
                           list is displayed. List boxes are created using the `JList`
                           component. See also **combo box**, **selectable list**.

list components   A collective term for the two components that provide a one-
                           column arrangement of data. See also **list box**, **selectable
                           list**.

look and feel   The appearance and behavior of a complete set of GUI
                           components. See also **Java look and feel**.

MDI   (multiple document interface) An interface style in which
                           primary windows are represented as internal frames inside a
                           backing window.

measured-progress   A progress bar that shows how much of an operation is
bar   complete. See also **indeterminate-progress bar**,
                           progress bar.

menu   A list of choices (menu items) logically grouped and
                           displayed by an application so that a user need not
                           memorize all available commands or options. Menus in the
                           Java look and feel are "sticky"—that is, they remain posted
                           on screen after the user clicks the menu title. Menus are
                           created using the `JMenu` component. See also
                           contextual menu, **drop-down menu**, **menu bar**, **menu item**,
                           submenu.

menu bar   The horizontal strip at the top of a window that contains the titles of the application's drop-down menus. Menu bars are created using the `JMenuBar` component. See also **drop-down menu**.

menu item   A choice in a menu. Menu items (text or graphics) are typically commands or other options that a user can select. Menu items are created using the `JMenuItem` component.

menu separator   See **separator**.

middle mouse button   The central button on a three-button mouse (typically used in UNIX® environments). The Java look and feel does not utilize the middle mouse button. See also **mouse button 2**.

mnemonic   An underlined alphanumeric character, typically in a menu title, menu item, or the text of a button or component. A mnemonic shows the user which key to press (in conjunction with the Alt key) to activate a command or navigate to a component. See also **keyboard operations**, **keyboard shortcut**.

modal dialog box   In a JFC application, a dialog box that prevents the user's interaction with other windows in the current application. Modal dialog boxes are created using the `JDialog` component. See also **dialog box**, **modeless dialog box**.

modal secondary window   Prevents users from interacting with other windows of an application until that modal window is closed. (In contrast, a modeless secondary window does not prevent users from interacting with other windows.) See also **dialog box**, **modal dialog box**.

mode   A mode is an operational state to which a system has been switched. It implies that at least two states are available. The effects of a user's actions differ in different situations, or modes, defined in the application. Often, a mode lets users perform only certain actions.

modeless dialog box   In a JFC application, a dialog box whose presence does not prevent the user from interacting with other windows in the current application. Modeless dialog boxes are created using the `JDialog` component. See also **dialog box**, **modal dialog box**.

modifier key	A key (for example, the Control or the Shift key) that does not produce an alphanumeric character but rather modifies the meaning of other keys.
monitored-entities view	Displays an icon and alarm graphic for one or more monitored entities and their containers (if any).
monitored entity	An entity that the application monitors.
MRU list	(most recently used) In the File menu, a dynamic list of a user's most recently opened objects. Users can reopen these objects.
mouse button 1	The primary button on a mouse (the only button, for Macintosh users). By default, mouse button 1 is the leftmost button, though users might switch the button settings so that the rightmost button becomes mouse button 1. See also **middle mouse button**, **mouse button 2**.
mouse button 2	On a two-button or three-button mouse, the button that is used to display contextual menus. By default, mouse button 2 is the rightmost button on the mouse, though users might switch the settings so that the leftmost button becomes mouse button 2. On mouse devices with only one button, users get the effect of mouse button 2 by holding down the Control key when pressing mouse button 1. See also **contextual menu**, **middle mouse button**, **mouse button 1**.
mouse-over feedback	A change in the visual appearance of an interface element that occurs when the user moves the pointer over it—for example, the display of a button border when the pointer moves over a toolbar button.
multiple document interface	See **MDI**.
non-dedicated property window	Affects only objects that are currently selected. The window affects different objects if a user changes the selection while the property window is displayed. See also **property window**.
noneditable combo box	See **combo box**.

non-inspecting property window
Displays a static view, or "snapshot," of the selected object's property values—accurate as of the time that the property window opened. See also **property window**.

object
(1) In user interface design, a logical entity that an application presents in an interface and that users manipulate—for example, a document, chapter, or paragraph in a word- processing application, or a mail server, mailbox, or mail message in a mail program.

(2) In programming, the principal building block of object-oriented applications. Each object is a programming unit consisting of data (instance variables) and functions (instance classes). A component is a particular type of object. See **component**.

onset delay
For tool tips, the amount of time before a tool tip is displayed. See also **duration**, **tool tip**.

overview page
In wizards, provides an overview of the wizard's steps. Typically, an overview page is needed only in very complex wizards or in wizards that do not display a list of steps in the left pane of their pages.

pane
A collective term for icon panes, scroll panes, split panes, and tabbed panes.

panel
(1) A collective term for scroll panes, split panes, and tabbed panes.

(2) A container for organizing the contents of a window, dialog box, or applet. Panels are created using the JPanel component. See also **tabbed pane**.

password field
A special text field in which the user types a password. The field displays a masking character for each typed character. Password fields are created using the JPasswordField component.

perceived performance
Based on how fast an application seems to its users—that is, how well it responds to them, not necessarily how fast it fulfills their requests. See also **responsiveness**.

plain window	An unadorned window with no title bar or window controls, typically used for splash screens. Plain windows are created using the JWindow component. See also **primary window**, **window controls**.
pointer	A small graphic that moves around the screen as the user manipulates the mouse (or another pointing device). Depending on its location and the active application, the pointer can assume various shapes, such as an arrowhead, crosshair, or clock. By moving the pointer and pressing mouse buttons, a user can select objects, set the insertion point, and activate windows. Sometimes called the "cursor." See also **insertion point**, **pointer feedback**.
pointer feedback	Visual feedback provided by changing the shape of the pointer. See also **pointer**.
primary key	In a sorted table, the main column of values by which the table is sorted.
primary window	A top-level window of an application, where the principal interaction with the user occurs. The title bar and borders of primary windows always retain the look and feel of the user's native platform. Primary windows are created using the JFrame component. See also **dialog box**, **secondary window**.
progress animation	A progress bar or progress checklist that shows how much of an operation is complete or that an operation is in progress. See also **progress bar**.
progress bar	An interface element that indicates one or more operations are in progress and shows the user what proportion of the operations has been completed. Progress bars are created using the JProgressBar component. See also **control**, **slider**.
progress page	Provides feedback to users about progress of a wizard's current operation.
properties	For user interface objects, characteristics whose values users can view or change. See also **object**.

property window   Enables a user to display or change the characteristics of one or more objects, typically objects displayed in the parent window.

requirements page   In wizards, a type of page that describes what the user must know, do, or have in order to complete the wizard.

response delay   The length of time that a user must wait before an application acknowledges or fulfills a specific request from the user.

responsiveness   As defined by Jeff Johnson in his book, *GUI Bloopers: Don'ts and Do's for Software Developers and Web Designers*, responsiveness is "the software's ability to keep up with users and not make them wait."

row-selection model   A selection model in which users of a table cannot select a single cell without selecting that cell's entire row. See also **cell-selection model**, **selection model**.

row-selection table   A table in which selecting a cell also selects that cell's entire row. See also **cell-selection table**.

row striping   In tables, the technique of using one background color for even-numbered rows and a different background color for odd-numbered rows.

scalability   (1) An application's ability to let users easily find, view, and manipulate widely varying numbers of objects.

(2) As an aspect of performance, the ability of an application to work under heavy loads—for example, large numbers of concurrent users or large sets of data.

scroll arrow   In a scrollbar, one of the arrows that a user can click to move through displayed information in the corresponding direction (up or down in a vertical scrollbar, left or right in a horizontal scrollbar). See also **scrollbar**.

scroll box

A box that a user can drag in the channel of a scrollbar to cause scrolling in the corresponding direction. The scroll box's position in the scrollbar indicates the user's location in the list, window, or pane. In the Java look and feel, the scroll box's size indicates what proportion of the total information is currently visible on screen. A large scroll box, for example, indicates that the user can peruse the contents with just a few clicks in the scrollbar. See also **scrollbar**.

scroll pane

A container that provides scrolling with optional vertical and horizontal scrollbars. Scroll panes are created using the JScrollPane component. See also **scrollbar**.

scrollbar

A component that enables a user to control what portion of a document or list (or similar information) is visible on screen. A scrollbar consists of a vertical or horizontal channel, a scroll box that moves through the channel of the scrollbar, and two scroll arrows. Scrollbars are created using the JScrollBar component. See also **scroll arrow**, **scroll box**, **scroll pane**.

searching

An application feature that lets users specify which objects in a set will be displayed in a window, based on the user's criteria, called a query. See also **filtering**.

secondary window

A modal or modeless window created from and dependent upon a primary window. Secondary windows set options or supply additional details about actions and objects in the primary window. Secondary windows are dismissed when their associated primary window is dismissed. Secondary windows are created using either the JDialog component (for dialog boxes and utility windows) or the JOptionPane component (for alert boxes). See also **alert box**, **dialog box**, **primary window**.

selectable list

A one-column arrangement of data in which the items that users select from the list are designated for a subsequent action. Command buttons can operate on this selection. When another selection is made, any previous selection in the selectable list is deselected. Selectable lists are created using the JList component. See also **list box**.

select
(1) In user interface design, refers narrowly to designating one or more objects, typically for a subsequent action. UI components are *activated* while user objects are *selected*.

(2) In technical documentation, refers generally to the action of clicking list items, checkboxes, radio buttons, and so forth. See also **activation, choose**.

selection model
In a table, a set of rules and techniques for selecting a portion of the table, such as a cell or row. See also **editing model**.

separator
A line graphic that is used to divide components into logical groupings. Separators are created using the `JSeparator` component.

server
A network device that manages resources and supplies services to a client. See also **client**.

slider
A control that enables the user to set a value in a range — for example, the RGB values for a color. Sliders are created using the `JSlider` component.

sort indicator
A small triangular graphic that, when displayed in the header of a table column, indicates that the column is sorted and whether the sort is ascending or descending.

sort key
In tables, a column by which a table is sorted.

split pane
A container that enables the user to adjust the relative size of two adjacent panes. Split panes are created using the `JSplitPane` component.

stable sort
A sort in which previously sorted rows (if any) retain their positions relative to one another, if they have identical values in the new sort column.

standalone wizard
A wizard that users can start directly — for example, from a desktop icon, a command line, or a file viewer. See also **wizard, standalone wizard**.

status animation
An animation indicating only that an operation is in progress, not how much of it is complete. See also **progress animation**.

status bar	An area at the bottom of a primary window. A status bar is used to display status messages and read-only information about the object that the window represents. See also **object**, **primary window**.
submenu	A menu that is displayed when a user chooses an associated menu item in a higher-level menu. (Such menu items are identified by a rightward-facing triangle.) Submenus are created using the JMenu component.
summary page	An optional page that summarizes the work a wizard has performed and lists any actions users should take after closing the wizard.
tabbed pane	A container that enables the user to switch between several components (usually JPanel components) that appear to share the same space on screen. The user can view a particular panel by clicking its tab. Tabbed panes are created using the JTabbedPane component.
table	A two-dimensional arrangement of data in rows and columns. Tables are created using the JTable component.
task analysis	The process of observing users as they work. The goal of the process is to discover which tasks make up the user's work and how best to facilitate those tasks through an application's user interface.
text area	A multiline region for displaying (and sometimes editing) text. Text in such areas is restricted to a single font, size, and style. Text areas are created using the JTextArea component.
text field	An area that displays a single line of text. In a noneditable text field, a user can copy, but not change, the text. In an editable text field, a user can type new text or edit the existing text. Text fields are created using the JTextField component. See also **password field**.
title bar	The strip at the top of a window that contains its title and window controls. See also **window controls**.

toggle button   A button that alternates between two states. For example, a user might click one toggle button in a toolbar to turn italics on and off. A single toggle button has checkbox behavior; a programmatically grouped set of toggle buttons can be given the mutually exclusive behavior of radio buttons. Toggle buttons are created using the `JToggleButton` component. See also **checkbox**, **toolbar button**.

tool tip   Small rectangles of short text strings that appear on screen to provide information about a component or area whenever the pointer is over that area.

toolbar   A collection of frequently used commands or options. Toolbars typically contain buttons, but other components (such as text fields and combo boxes) can be placed in toolbars as well. Toolbars are created using the `JToolBar` component. See also **toolbar button**.

toolbar button   A button that appears in a toolbar, typically a command or toggle button. A toolbar button can also display a menu. Toolbar buttons are created using the `JButton` or `JToggleButton` component. See also **command button**, **toggle button**.

top-level object type   For a window, the type of user-interface object that the window represents, such as a file, a mailbox, or a computer. See also **object** (1).

tool palette   An internal utility window whose buttons enable users to choose a tool, such as a paint brush, from a set of tools. See also **utility window**.

tree component   A representation of hierarchical data (for example, directory and file names) as a graphical outline. Clicking expands or collapses elements of the outline. Tree components are created using the `JTree` component.

tree table   A table in which the leftmost column is a tree of objects, one object to a row, and the other columns consist of rows that describe the corresponding object in the tree.

turner   A graphic used in the tree component. The user clicks a turner to expand or collapse a container in the hierarchy.

unavailable   Not applicable in the current system state. When a component is unavailable, it appears dimmed and is skipped by keyboard navigation.

user-input pages   In wizards, user-input pages enable users to customize how a wizard performs its task. Each wizard has at least two user-input pages and can have as many such pages as are needed for the task.

utility window   A modeless window that typically displays a collection of tools, colors, fonts, or patterns. User choices made in a utility window affect whichever primary window is active. A utility window is not dismissed when a primary window is dismissed. Utility windows are created using the `JDialog` component. See also **tool palette**, **secondary window**.

view   A specific visual representation of information in a window or pane.

wait pointer   Indicates that an operation is in progress and that the user cannot perform other tasks.

window   A user interface element that organizes and contains the information that users see in an application. See also **dialog box**, **plain window**, **primary window**, **secondary window**, **utility window**.

window controls   Controls that affect the state of a window (for example, the Maximize button in Microsoft Windows title bars).

wizard   A window that leads a user through a task one step at a time—requesting a series of responses from the user and then performing the task based on those responses.

INDEX

(Continued)

(Continued)

Colophon

LEAD WRITER
Marcus Jordan

LEAD HUMAN INTERFACE DESIGNERS
Robin Jeffries and Chip Alexander

EDITOR
Louise Galindo

GRAPHIC DESIGNER AND COVER ILLUSTRATION
Coleen Baik

COVER DESIGN
Bruce G. Lee and Coleen Baik

GUIDELINE CONTRIBUTORS
David-John Burrowes, Helen Cunningham, Jeff Dunn, Brian Ehret,
Martine Freiberger, George Kaempf, Kim O'Brien, Nils Pedersen,
Teresa Roberts, Tom Spine, Kristin Travis, Harry Vertelney

Special thanks to Jeff Johnson for his insights on responsive
applications and to Chris Ryan for designing the Java
look and feel.

Grateful acknowledgments to Michael Albers, Eileen Bugee,
Patria Brown, Sue Factor, Dave Mendenhall, Kartik Mithal,
Lynn Monsanto, Bob Silva, Jenny Shum, Maya Venkatraman,
Andrea Vine, Steve Wilson, the Sun Online Visual Evangelists,
and the 85 reviewers of this book's preliminary drafts.

This book was written on Sun Microsystems workstations using
Adobe® FrameMaker software. Line art was created using Adobe®
Illustrator. Screen shots were edited in Adobe® Photoshop.

Text type is SunSans and bullets are ITC Zapf Dingbats. Courier is
used for computer voice.